Of Mirrors & Apple Trees

Of Mirrors & Apple Trees

The Lomdus of Peru u-Revu

Rabbi Ephraim Meth

KODESH PRESS

© Ephraim Meth 2014
ISBN 978-0692338032

All rights reserved. Except for brief quotations in printed reviews, no part of this publication may be reproduced, stored in a retrieval system, or transmitted in any form or by any means (printed, written, photocopied, visual electronic, audio, or otherwise) without the prior permissions of the publisher.

Published & Distributed by
Kodesh Press L.L.C.
New York, NY
kodeshpress@gmail.com

The Jewish women had mirrors, which they used for cosmetics, and they brought these mirrors as donations to the mishkan. *Moshe was appalled, because such mirrors are associated with the evil inclination. But Hashem told him, "Accept them, since they are more precious to me than all the other donations, since the women used them to conceive many multitudes in Egypt."*

When their husbands were weary with back-breaking labor, they would go and bring them food and drink, and feed them. Then, each woman would look at herself and her husband in a mirror, and speak persuasively to him, teasing, "I am more beautiful than you," and they would thereby arouse their husband's passion, and they would make themselves available to their husbands. They would conceive there, and they would give birth there. This is what the verse refers to when it says, "I aroused you beneath the apple tree" (Shir ha-Shirim 8:5).

The kiyor, *whose function was to ensure marital harmony, was fashioned with these mirrors.*

— Rashi, Shemos 38:8

The following letter was penned by my rebbe, Rabbi Michael Rosensweig, for my first sefer, *Kuntres Sha'ashuei Ephraim* on *Maseches Chullin*. The letter is reproduced here with Rabbi Rosensweig's blessing.

I was delighted to receive the manuscript that my student, Ephraim Meth, is about to publish. Despite his young age, Ephraim is already renowned both within our Yeshiva and outside of it as someone unique, for his diligence, for his knowledge, and for his depth of understanding. Even a quick glance at this book offers sufficient evidence to its author's unique talents and to his ability to analyze a topic with wisdom and good taste.

I have no doubt that the world of Torah students will appreciate this book. May the author continue to grow higher and higher in Torah study and in fear of heaven, and may he merit placing more of his original thoughts on the "table of kings," i.e., the rabbinic table.

Written and signed with the Torah's blessing,

Rabbi Michael Rosensweig

Rosh Yeshiva and Rosh Kollel
Yeshivas Rabbeinu Yitzchak Elchanan

Table of Contents

Introduction 13

1. *Tzaddikim* Who Neglected Procreation 20

2. Genetics & Eugenics 28

3. Adulthood 36

4. Marriage 44

5. Intercourse 51

6. *Sirus* 63

7. *Hotza'as Zera le-Vatalah* 68

8. Man & Woman 74

9. Old & Young 80

10. Jew & Gentile 90

Conclusion 95

Index 97

Introduction

The entirety of Jewish ideology, philosophy, ethics, and theology is reflected in the Talmud and *halakhah*. The lessons and ideas elucidated by these genres can be derived with equal clarity by analyzing the telos (purpose) of the *mitzvos* and their laws. Moreover, proper understanding of the *mitzvos*' telos informs pursuit of *chasidus*, since *chasidus* means actualizing the spirit of the *mitzvos* and their laws even when the laws' letter does not require it.

Proper understanding of the *mitzvos*' telos also helps us determine their scope. It is true that the admonition against *darshinan ta'ama di-Kra* (lit., "seeking the reason for a verse") adjures us from expanding or limiting the scope of a law based on speculation or supposition about its telos. However, this admonition does not prevent us from doing so based on concrete hermeneutic evidence about its telos. Neither Rishonim nor Acharonim shied away from determining, when appropriate, the scope of a mitzvah based on concrete evidence about its purpose. For instance, the Rambam[1] rules that the prohibition against intermarriage applies

---
1. *Hilchos Issurei Bi'ah* 12:1, as interpreted by *Lechem Mishneh* to *Hilchos Malveh ve-Loveh* 3:1.

not only to the seven Canaanite nations, but to all gentile nations, because women from any gentile nation will lead their husbands and children away from Hashem and His values. Similarly, the Rashba[2] rules that "the prohibition against *sirus* after *sirus* is a *gezeiras ha-Kasuv* [a Scriptural decree] *and the ta'ama di-kra is...* that it is not apparent that the subject of this *sirus* was previously sterilized." An extensive analysis of this Rashba can be found in chapter six. R. Mayer Twersky[3] demonstrates that the *Sefer ha-Chinnuch* regularly employed teleology to determine a mitzvah's scope. An example of this, not discussed by R. Twersky, can also be found in chapter six.

R. Netanel Wiederblank[4] cites numerous other examples of this phenomenon, but argues that we only endorse teleological analysis of a mitzvah's scope when logical intuition and the biblical text's simple meaning (*peshuto shel mikra*) support that analysis. However, since "logical intuition" and "simple meaning" are largely subjective criteria, which have not been extensively defined by halakhists, they cannot serve as predictive criteria for when to admit teleology into the domain of halakhic analysis and when to refuse it admission.

In contrast to R. Wiederblank, R. Mordechai Willig[5] suggests that we are not *doresh ta'ama di-Kra*, but we are *doresh ta'ama di-drashah* (seeking the reason for

---
2. *Shabbos* 111a.
3. "Halakhic Axiology Within the *Sefer ha-Hinnukh*." *Tradition* 37:3.
4. "*Tafkid ha-Sevara be-Kevi'as Dinim de-Oraisa*." *Beis Yitzchak* 40, pp. 405-425.
5. Cited by R. Wiederblank, ibid. p. 425 fn. 52.

INTRODUCTION

a hermeneutically derived law). This pithy yet highly significant statement alludes to the theory described above: when numerous *derashos* reveal laws whose common denominator is a particular telos, we may expand or limit a mitzvah's scope based on that telos.

Every chapter of this book demonstrates the principle of *darshinan ta'ama di-drashah*; indeed, the book can be viewed as an extended proof of this principle's validity, of its acceptance by Rishonim, Acharonim, and Poskim. For instance, chapter four addresses how the multiple overlapping purposes of institutionalized marriage impact on the laws of marriage; chapter five discusses how the telos of *bi'ah* and the telos of various *bi'ah*-dependent imperatives and prohibitions (e.g., *kiddushin*, *yibbum*, procreation, *issurei bi'ah*) impact the halakhic definition of *bi'ah*; chapters six and seven discuss how the potential purposes for prohibiting *hotza'as zera le-vatalah* and *sirus* help determine when these respective actions are forbidden and when they are permitted; and chapter eight explores five potential purposes for having children and their impact on women's marital rights.

This book's title underwent a number of revisions. Originally, the manuscript was called "Torah Perspectives on Human Reproduction." Next, it was called "Torah Perspectives on Procreation." Finally, it obtained its present title, *Of Mirrors & Apple Trees: The Lomdus of Peru u-Revu*. What concerns informed these revisions?

First, the book's subject matter is extremely difficult to render in English with *tzenius*, proper discretion and sensitivity. The Rambam[6] writes that *lashon ha-kodesh*, the holy tongue, is so called because it contains no term that uniquely refers to private matters; such matters are only mentioned euphemistically in *lashon ha-kodesh*. In writing this book, there was concern lest readers be justly offended by the book's terminology. Even the term "human reproduction" seemed too explicit, and was therefore changed first to "procreation," then to *"peru u-revu."* Similarly, every effort was made to avoid indiscreet references to private matters. Many explicit terms were replaced with more discreet words, and some were replaced with Hebrew terms. These replacements, however, may fluster readers unfamiliar with talmudic terminology.

Second, this book belongs neither to the genre of ideology nor to the genre of practical *halakhah*. It belongs to the genre colloquially known as *lomdus*, analysis of how characteristics of concepts or things relate to one another. "Torah perspectives" would have suggested an ideological book; *"The Lomdus of Peru u-Revu* indicates that it is not ideological, but analytic.

Because this is not a book of ideology, this book consistently avoids citing aggadic portions of the Talmud or *sifrei machshavah* (books of Jewish thought) as evidence for its theses. As mentioned at this introduction's outset, the entirety of Jewish thought corresponds to *halakhos*, concrete laws. Every lesson

---

6. See Ramban to *Shemos* 30:13.

Introduction

taught by a Midrash, or by a book of philosophy or *musar*, could be equally taught by properly analyzing a *halakhah*. This book arrives at its conclusions by direct analysis of Jewish law. However, while the book quotes extensively from Jewish law, it is not a book of practical *halakhah*. It does not confer the imprimatur of *halakhah le-ma'aseh*, permission to implement the law in practice, on every opinion it cites. Quite the contrary, it cites many opinions that were voiced by renowned authorities, yet were rejected by consensus. The purpose of citing these opinions is to help understand the conceptual underpinnings of a law or mitzvah, the *lomdus* of that law, not to give the reader guidance for practically structuring his or her life. Although we try to note the consensus opinion regarding each contemporary issue discussed, some issues may have been overlooked. Therefore, the reader is advised to consult his or her Posek for any issue that arises, and not to rely on this book to inform practical halakhic decisions.

Moreover, as a book of *lomdus*, this book is meant for serious study, not for light reading.

Talmudists traditionally engage in two types of analysis. The first, textual analysis, is most important, because all our values must be rooted in the traditional texts. Yet textual analysis is most difficult to convey in English, rooted as it is in nuances of traditional texts' Hebrew and Aramaic formulations. This book, written as it is in English, therefore focuses on the second type of analysis, conceptual analysis. This entails, among other things, investigating the possibility that many laws stem from a common denominator, and conversely, the possibility that discrepancies between rulings in two cases stem from the fact that each case contains characteristics not present in the other.

Moreover, "perspectives" would have suggested that the book merely culls or translates the opinions of others. While the book is entirely faithful to the rulings, explanations, and *weltanschauung* of *gedolei ha-dor* past and present, and comes close to comprehensively surveying the range of mainstream opinions pertaining to each topic, each chapter is primarily a *chiddush*, a novel thought that is deeply rooted in traditional sources and helps us understand those sources with greater depth, breadth of perspective, and clarity.

On a personal note, when my wife and I first learned about the obstacles in our path to procreation, it became painful to think about children. Although we tried not to think about them, like the proverbial pink elephant, we could not avoid such thoughts. And so, just as R. Chaim Soloveitchik would study the laws of death when beset by the fear of death, I turned to the Torah's treatment of procreation when confronted by fear of childlessness. This book's spiritual roots are embedded in those moments of loneliness and struggle, even though the book's research and writing came much later. Baruch Hashem, our sojourn with infertility was blessedly brief. Yet to the soul in distress,

Introduction

each moment is an eternity. We have not forgotten, and *b'li neder*, will not forget the pain. This book is dedicated to Hashem, in heartfelt thanks for our son Michoel, and in prayer that He grant all Jewish families happiness and progeny.

Chapter 1

Tzaddikim Who Neglected Procreation

This chapter will discuss four righteous men who partially or totally neglected *peru u-revu*, and the lessons that classical commentaries derive from their conduct.

Yosef ha-Tzaddik neglected *peru u-revu*, since the *Shulchan Aruch*[7] writes that one should ideally marry at age twelve or thirteen, while Yosef was still unmarried at seventeen.[8] Moshe Rabbeinu partially neglected *peru u-revu*, since the Mishnah[9] says that one must father a boy and a girl, while Moshe fathered two boys but no girls.[10] King Chizkiyahu initially neglected *peru u-revu* and did not marry, since he foresaw with divine inspiration that his children would be wicked. Ultimately, Yeshayahu ha-Navi rebuked him, so he married and had children.[11] Finally, Ben Azzai completely neglected *peru u-revu*, claiming that he desired Torah too much,

---

7. *Even ha-Ezer* 1:3.
8. *Bereishis* 37:2.
9. *Yevamos* 61b.
10. Ibid.
11. *Berachos* 10a.

and that others could engage in populating the world.¹² This chapter will survey some classical responses to these four paragons' behavior, focusing particularly on how *peru u-revu* differs from the other *mitzvos* of the Torah. The chapter will conclude by analyzing how the idiosyncrasies of *peru u-revu* relate to one another, and this analysis will yield a heretofore underemphasized yet fundamental insight into the character of *peru u-revu*.

Poskim adopt four approaches to explain the apparently antinomian conduct of these righteous individuals. First, perhaps they neglected *peru u-revu* due to extenuating or exceptional circumstances. For instance, the *Aruch ha-Shulchan*¹³ writes that Ben Azzai was excused from *peru u-revu* since he would have died from anguish over the disruption of his Torah study engendered by marriage and parenting. Similarly, R. Elchanan Wasserman¹⁴ writes that Ben Azzai loved Torah so much that he was psychologically incapable of disrupting his studies for *peru u-revu*. In talmudic language, his exemption from the mitzvah is known as *oneis rachmana patrei*, the Merciful One exempts someone who cannot help himself. Moreover, Beis Hillel explains that Moshe neglected *peru u-revu* because Hashem commanded it, thereby excusing him from his obligation.¹⁵ Similarly, R. Wosner¹⁶ writes that King

---

12. *Yevamos* 63b.
13. *Even ha-Ezer* 1:4.
14. *Kovetz He'aros, hosafah* 1.
15. *Yevamos* 62a.
16. *Shut Shevet ha-Levi* 4:161.

Chizkiyahu knew with nearly prophetic certainty that his children would be wicked, while we, even with modern science and statistics, can never attain that level of certainty. According to this approach, *peru u-revu* is no different than the Torah's other *mitzvos*.

The second approach argues that even if these paragons' neglect or delay of *peru u-revu* was less than ideal, it still was not reprehensible. Although Moshe Rabbeinu had no daughters, he had sons, and therefore fulfilled half the *mitzvah*. For this reason, even though the courts must compel childless men to have children, they do not compel men with one child, who fulfilled half the *mitzvah*, to have more children.[17] Similarly, Yosef ha-Tzaddik did not neglect *peru u-revu*; he merely delayed his fulfillment of the *mitzvah*. For this reason, we nowadays permit Torah students to delay marriage past age twenty, even though we do not permit Torah students to delay other, less constantly incumbent *mitzvos*.[18] In addition, we uphold oaths to postpone marriage, since such oaths do not negate *mitzvas peru u-revu*, while we do not uphold oaths to never marry, since such oaths do negate *mitzvas peru u-revu*.[19] Furthermore, Ben Azzai correctly noted that not every man must participate in procreation to satisfy the telos of *peru u-revu*; the mitzvah is "possible at others' hands."[20] Finally, the *Minchas Chinnuch*[21] writes that one

---

17. *Yevamos* 64a; see *Shut Me'il Tzedakah* 33.
18. Rambam, *Hilchos Ishus* 15:2.
19. *Shut ha-Rashba* 4:91.
20. *Yevamos* 63b.
21. *Minchas Chinnuch* 1.

who attempts to fulfill *peru u-revu* is never guaranteed success, and all one's efforts are a prerequisite to the mitzvah rather than a fulfillment of the mitzvah. For this reason, one who delays or neglects *peru u-revu* has not truly neglected the mitzvah's fulfillment, but has merely postponed a prerequisite that anyhow could not guarantee the mitzvah's fulfillment.

The third approach declares these paragons' behaviors normative, and adjusts the parameters of *peru u-revu* based on their behavior. Hence, the *Derech Pikkudecha*[22] writes that when one is not troubled by inappropriate thoughts, he may delay his marriage, like Yosef, until age seventeen or eighteen. Similarly, the Rambam[23] writes that one may delay marriage until age seventeen or twenty in order to accumulate Torah knowledge. R. Asher Weiss further suggests that one may delay marriage until he attains the physical, cognitive, and emotional maturity necessary to successfully head a household, and until he obtains sufficient capital or skills to support a family.[24] Along these lines, the Rambam[25] and *Shulchan Aruch*[26] codify Ben Azzai's behavior as normative for anyone whose spirit, like Ben Azzai's, constantly desires Torah. The Maharshal,[27] in a ruling not accepted by later authorities, writes that a woman may ingest contraceptive potions

---

22. Cited in *Tur* (Mechon Yerushalayim), p. 3, fn. 13.
23. *Hilchos Ishus* 15:2.
24. *Minchas Asher* to *Bereishis*, pp. 13-17.
25. *Hilchos Ishus* 15:3.
26. *Even ha-Ezer* 1:4.
27. *Yam Shel Shlomo, Yevamos* 6:44.

if she fears, like King Chizkiyahu, that her children will be wicked. Finally, the *Shut Avnei Nezer*[28] rules that one who, like Moshe Rabbeinu, had two sons but no daughters, nevertheless has fulfilled the mitzvah of *peru u-revu*, at least *bediered*.

The fourth approach pertains uniquely to King Chizkiyahu. Chizkiyahu's conduct is absolutely regarded as not normative since he was censured by Yeshayahu ha-Navi: "What business have you with the Merciful One's secrets; you should do what is incumbent upon you, and the Holy One, blessed be He, will do what He desires."[29]

Yet Poskim dispute the scope of the prohibition against imitating King Chizkiyahu. R. Menashe Klein,[30] in a minority opinion, forbids pre-marital genetic testing, at least after a couple began to date seriously or got engaged, since we should not postpone, jeopardize, or change our mode of fulfilling *peru u-revu* based on dismaying knowledge about the future: "What business have we with the Merciful One's secrets?" Although most Poskim[31] permit and even encourage pre-marital genetic testing, they forbid women who fear that their children will be wicked from taking contraceptive medication.[32] Moreover, although R. Moshe Shternbuch[33] permits two parents who are both

---

28. *Even ha-Ezer* 1.
29. *Berachos* 10a.
30. *Shut Mishneh Halachos* 12:265.
31. Cited by R. Klein, ibid.
32. *Shut Shevet ha-Levi* 4:161.
33. *Shut Teshuvos ve-Hanhagos* 1:890.

Tzaddikim Who Neglected Procreation

carriers of a genetic disease to remain married and practice contraception, R. Yitzchok Weiss[34] expresses uncertainty about this leniency and urges the couple to either remain married without contraception or to separate. Just as King Chizkiyahu could not interfere with "the Merciful One's secrets" and withhold a wicked son from the world, we may not interfere with "the Merciful One's secrets" and withhold a severely ill child from the world.

As an aside, having touched upon the topic of contraceptives and birth control, it behooves us to clarify the rabbinic consensus about how to practically approach this issue. Upon submitting the first draft of this book for review, I received two radically different reactions to its treatment of birth control. One reviewer, a prominent doctor, recalled patients who had many children in as many years, and, on account of the stress of child-rearing, sometimes lost control of themselves and fought with their spouses or hit their children. These patients were initially convinced, erroneously, that all contraceptive techniques were forbidden, and they therefore did not even bother to ask their rabbi about birth control. Recounting numerous similar stories, the doctor who reviewed this manuscript urged me to encourage my readers to ask their rabbis about birth control's permissibility.

A second reviewer, the assistant rabbi of a major synagogue, recounted how couples took contraceptives for the first three years of their marriage solely for

---

34. *Shut Minchas Yitzchak* 3:26 and 6:144.

personal convenience, which is surely an illegitimate motive to delay fulfillment of a mitzvah. This reviewer urged me to encourage my readers to clarify with their rabbis the potential prohibitions involved in birth control. Many birth control techniques are forbidden under all circumstances, and many circumstances offer insufficient grounds to permit any type of birth control. Moreover, many intangible factors inform the decision about whether birth control is permitted or forbidden, and the presence or absence of these factors can only be assessed by a rabbi who possesses broad experience in human relations and deeply accurate knowledge-based halakhic intuition.

The common denominator of these two responses, which reflects the rabbinic consensus on the issue, is: make no assumptions about the permissibility or prohibition of birth control in a given circumstance; instead, ask your rabbi.

This discussion yields the following conclusion. *Peru u-revu* is an idiosyncratic mitzvah, and its idiosyncrasy has both lenient and stringent consequences. *Peru u-revu* requires more maturity than most *mitzvos*, and consumes more assets and energy than most *mitzvos*. Hence, we are lenient, and allow people to postpone *peru u-revu* until they attain the maturity and resources to properly fulfill the mitzvah. Yet once they are ready to procreate, we cannot easily exempt them from *peru u-revu* on the grounds that the mitzvah's financial or emotional toll is too great, such as when the couple wants to avoid raising genetically ill children. Moreover, pursuit of *peru u-revu* does not guarantee fulfillment of *peru u-revu*. This results in leniencies wherein exceptional individuals may delay or neglect pursuing the mitzvah, but it also results in stringencies, since we cannot abandon the mitzvah out of concern for the probability of ill or sinful progeny. In addition, *peru u-revu* is a constant mitzvah, not limited to a specific span of time, and, although we cannot and should not pursue its fulfillment in every waking moment, it is nonetheless unceasingly incumbent upon us. It is a mitzvah that must be fulfilled by any and every man. Yet for this reason, some individuals and some times can be excused from the mitzvah, since other men at other times can fulfill it. The very idiosyncrasies that make *peru u-revu* so stringent may give rise to its leniencies and exceptions.

Chapter 2

Genetics & Eugenics

Eugenics has two fundamental components. First, the goal of eugenics is to eliminate "negative" physical, cognitive, emotional, or spiritual traits from a given population, and to propagate "positive" traits in that population.[35] Second, the modus operandi of eugenics includes public relations campaigns, legislation against undesirable unions, and, in extreme cases, sterilization, incarceration, or murder of individuals with traits deemed undesirable by eugenicists.[36] Historically, eugenics has been peripherally associated with ideologies such as social Darwinism and movements such as Planned Parenthood.[37] This chapter will address whether *halakhah* concurs with the goal and with the modus operandi of eugenics, and if so, to what extent. In particular, it will analyze halakhic approaches to genetic screening and to the prohibition of a *mamzer* marrying Jews with ordinary ancestry.

At first glance, the Torah's laws seem at least partially consistent with eugenic values. Ramban[38] explains that

---

35. See Edwin Black, *War Against the Weak*, pp. 9-19.
36. Ibid. p. 19.
37. Ibid. and pp. 125-144.
38. *Vayikra* 18:6.

people may not marry their close relatives (i.e., sisters, mothers, daughters, etc.), in order to avoid sickly offspring and to instead proliferate healthy children. Expanding on this, many contemporary authorities[39] rule that one should not marry any relative with whom, according to modern science, one has a higher than ordinary chance of conceiving sickly offspring. Furthermore, Dr. Avraham Abraham[40] opines that the Torah looks favorably on eradicating disease and promoting health via genetic engineering, since this is for the good of mankind. These sources indicate that *halakhah* desires to eradicate the "negative" trait of illness from our population group.

Along similar lines, the Talmud[41] records that two excessively tall, short, dark-complexioned, or light-complexioned individuals should not mate, lest their child be extremely different from his or her peers. Moreover, the Talmud[42] rules that one should not choose a spouse from a family of epileptics or of lepers, lest his or her child be an epileptic or a leper. Dr. Avraham Steinberg[43] asks: why does the *Shulchan Aruch*[44] codify the latter ruling, but not the former? Perhaps the answer lies in the fact that the

---

39. *Shut Be'er Moshe* 6:159-160. See also the sources cited by Dr. Avraham Steinberg, *Encyclopedia Hilchatis Refu'is*, vol. 7, p. 780, fn. 138.
40. *Nishmas Avraham* CM 425:1.
41. *Bechoros* 45b.
42. *Yevamos* 62b.
43. *Encyclopedia Hilchatis Refu'is*, ibid. p. 783, fn. 152.
44. *Even ha-Ezer* 2:7.

former set of marriages would only affect the child's social life, but would not affect the child's chances of survival. Legislation against such marriages cannot carry halakhic weight. In contrast, the latter set of marriages would affect the child's chances of survival, and are therefore forbidden by the halakhic directive to preserve and prolong life.

This distinction between life-saving and non-life-saving genetic legislation may inform the practice of some religious genetic testing organizations, which test only for life-threatening genetic illnesses, and not for other illnesses.

On the other hand, R. Moshe Feinstein,[45] in his endorsement of the genetic testing organization called Dor Yeshorim, makes clear that the purpose of genetic testing and avoidance of genetically problematic marriages is not to perfect the human species; rather, the purpose of these practices is to spare parents from pain and unborn children from death. Perhaps for this reason, R. Feinstein[46] writes that carriers of genetic diseases should not abstain from *peru u-revu*, but rather should marry fertile women, even though their offspring would have a fifty percent chance of suffering from debilitating genetic disease. Since *peru u-revu* obligates men to endure pain, even excessive pain, for the sake of having children, the potential father may not abstain from *peru u-revu* simply to avoid pain.

---

45. *Igros Moshe, Even ha-Ezer* 4:10; see also *Igros Moshe, Even ha-Ezer* 4:71.
46. Ibid., *Even ha-Ezer* 4:73.

While R. Feinstein seems to assign halakhically neutral value to the project of eliminating disease from mankind, R. Menashe Klein,[47] in his minority opinion not accepted by the consensus of contemporary rabbinic authorities, takes a more astonishing approach. R. Klein opposes genetic testing on principle, since we cannot determine whether conceiving an ill child advances or sets back the perfection of the cosmos. Such determinations should be made solely by Hashem, and humans should innocently commit themselves to His caring hands. Although R. Klein's opinion is not accepted by his colleagues, the fact that such an erudite scholar could maintain such an opinion demonstrates the extent to which "perfection of the species" as a human goal is foreign to Torah *weltanschauung*.

R. Shmuel Wosner[48] also seems opposed to genetic engineering, although the degree of his opposition is unclear. R. Wosner opposed genetic alteration of fish that would give scales to non-kosher fish. He cites the Ramban's[49] comment that the prohibition against interbreeding animal and plant species is based on the assumption that Hashem's creation is perfect and that we should therefore refrain from excessively tampering with it. Dr. Avraham Steinberg[50] interprets R. Wosner's ruling as evidence of reluctance to condone genetic engineering of any sort.

---

47. *Shut Mishneh Halachos* 12:265.
48. *Shut Shevet ha-Levi* 7:121.
49. *Vayikra* 19:19.
50. *Encyclopedia Hilchatis Refu'is*, ibid., p. 784, fn. 161.

The second phase of our analysis addresses the status of a *mamzer* in *halakhah*. How can we understand the *mamzer*'s prohibition against marrying a Jew of ordinary ancestry, and his permission to marry a female *mamzer*? Does the prohibition constitute legislation to inhibit his reproduction, and the permission merely a concession to make his life minimally tolerable? Or does the prohibition constitute a symbolic enactment, while the permission shows we are not interested in inhibiting the reproduction of *mamzerim*?

R. Samson Raphael Hirsch[51] writes that the *mamzer*'s prohibition to marry symbolizes that we seek spiritual purity and redeemed intimate life within the covenantal community. R. Hirsch clearly is not concerned about the *mamzer* bequeathing deficient traits to its offspring. Similarly, the *Sefer ha-Chinnuch*[52] writes that the *mamzer*'s marriage prohibition punishes the *mamzer*'s sinful parents and deters society at large from engaging in future sinful relationships. For this reason, a gentile who, had he been born to Jewish parents, would have been considered a *mamzer*, who subsequently converts, may marry ancestrally ordinary Jews, and is not presumed to possess defective traits due to the circumstances of his conception.

Moreover, the *Minchas Chinnuch*[53] entertains the possibility that if an ordinary man performs *yibbum* with

---

51. *Devarim* 23:3.
52. Mitzvah 560.
53. Ibid.

a female *mamzer*, their offspring would not be a *mamzer*. In this case, the mitzvah of *yibbum* offsets the *mamzer*'s ancestors' sin. Similarly, the *Piskei Teshuvos*[54] wonders whether or not the *mamzer*'s restrictions are lifted when his or her parents repent of their sin. Both of these suppositions, however, are rejected by mainstream *halakhah*. Still, the Rambam[55] suggests that a *mamzer* who engages in extra-marital relations with an ancestral Jew is punished less severely than a *mamzer* who engages in such relations within the context of marriage to an ancestral Jew. Clearly, the punishment was not aimed primarily at preventing *mamzerim* from reproducing, but rather was aimed, probably for symbolic reasons, solely at preventing *mamzerim* from marrying.

In contrast, the *Sefer ha-Chinnuch*[56] suggests a second approach, one that is more harmonious with eugenics: *mamzerim* possess defective spiritual or character traits that will be passed to their progeny, and therefore are prohibited from intermarrying with ancestral Jews. For this reason, even when the *mamzer* enters into a permissible relationship, such as when he or she marries another *mamzer* or a convert, his offspring still may not marry ancestral Jews. Moreover, the Tosafos[57] note that according to one rejected Tannaitic opinion, the Torah permits gentiles to engage in intercourse with Jews, yet at the same time, this opinion maintains that

---

54. Cited in R. Hershel Schachter, *Eretz ha-Tzvi*, p. 111.
55. *Hilchos Issurei Bi'ah* 15:2.
56. Mitzvah 560.
57. *Yevamos* 16b.

children born of such intercourse are *mamzerim*. Based on this, some Poskim[58] declare that if a married woman becomes pregnant via artificial insemination with the seed of someone other than her husband, her child is a *mamzer*, even though she did not engage in a forbidden act of intercourse. These Poskim clearly believe that the status of *mamzer* is not attendant on symbolism or sinfulness. Although some may have difficulty harmonizing modern science with this opinion of the *Sefer ha-Chinnuch*, the *Sefer ha-Chinnuch* is nevertheless conceptually important because it suggests that the Torah concurs with some goals of eugenics. Hence, the *Minchas Chinnuch*[59] contemplates the possibility that *mamzerim* are not commanded to reproduce, since Hashem does not desire the proliferation of *mamzerim*.

The genetics movement has great potential, and some of its advances, particularly genetic testing for hereditary diseases, have been embraced by contemporary halakhic authorities. Yet the Torah cautions us to refrain from excessive tampering with Hashem's creation, and against excessive hubris in determining what genetic advances will benefit humanity and what advances will not. It is unclear whether the *mamzer*'s marriage prohibition is designed to eliminate negative traits from our nation, and R. Feinstein did not invoke betterment of humanity as a rationale to permit genetic testing. As the progress of genetic technology marches

---

58. See R. Herschel Schachter, *Eretz ha-Tzvi*, p. 114.
59. Mitzvah 1.

on, we turn our eyes for guidance to the masters of talmudic tradition and bearers of the masoretic flame, the decisors whose authority is universally acknowledged, to the *gedolei ha-dor*.

Chapter 3

Adulthood

Do the ages of twelve and thirteen, when girls and boys transition out of childhood and begin adulthood, correspond to reproductive milestones? The Talmud[60] records a dispute seemingly about physiology, about whether or not an eleven-year-old girl is physiologically capable of conceiving and delivering a viable infant. The Talmud concludes that eleven-year-old girls are incapable of conceiving viable offspring. This ruling is significant for its conceptual ramifications, since it means that any girl who delivers a baby must already be an halakhic adult. In other words, once the girl's baby is delivered, the girl is obligated to perform *mitzvos* and is liable for her sins. However, Acharonim still debate whether the girl achieves adulthood because she reached reproductive maturity, or whether she reaches adulthood and reproductive maturity together on account of some other causal factor.

How should we understand the dissenting opinion's conceptual significance, that eleven-year-old girls are capable of delivering viable offspring? If a child is

---

60. *Yevamos* 12b, *Sanhedrin* 68b-69a.

physiologically capable of delivering viable offspring, we must concede that adulthood is not connected to reproductive maturity. After all, the child reached reproductive maturity and still did not halakhically transition into adulthood. Had this been true, it would have meant that even after the child's baby is delivered, the child is neither obligated to perform *mitzvos* nor liable to punishment for her sins.

Each party to the dispute about whether children are physiologically capable of reproducing has evidence for its position. For instance, a careful reading of Tanach should reveal that King David's wife Batsheva delivered King Shlomo when she was six years old, and that Calev, Uri, and Chur were each eight years old when they fathered their first son.[61] On the other hand, the Talmud[62] writes that if someone stole from a child convert who subsequently died, he need not search for his victim's heirs, since a child cannot have children.

Tosafos and R. Nissim each offer an explanation for this seemingly contradictory evidence. Tosafos[63] claim that people in the biblical era were able to have children at young ages, and therefore were halakhically deemed adults at younger ages. However, in the talmudic era, the minimum age for fertility increased. In both eras, anyone capable of having children was an adult; a child, by definition, cannot have children, and that is why one need not search for a child convert's

---

61. *Sanhedrin* 69b.
62. Ibid. 68b.
63. Ibid. 69a.

heirs. In contrast, R. Nissim[64] explains that nature did not change between the biblical and talmudic eras. Rather, most children cannot have children before ages twelve or thirteen, but a very few (*mi'uta de-mi'uta*) can have children at younger ages. Even though a child can have children, and hence adulthood is not a function of reproductive maturity, we need not be concerned that a child convert has heirs, since *halakhah* does not obligate us to be concerned about events with such low thresholds of probability. The *Birkas Avraham*[65] notes that, according to Tosafos, just as the threshold of adulthood changed between the biblical and talmudic eras, it may have changed between the talmudic era and contemporary times, while according to R. Nissim, that threshold of adulthood is static and remains constant in all eras.

R. Meir Simcha of Dvinsk[66] offers the following proof that reproductive maturity does not cause adulthood, but rather, the two merely correspond: sterile men and women can enter adulthood even though they cannot reproduce. R. Chaim Soloveitchik[67] responds that indeed, adulthood for the sterile is not caused by reproductive maturity. However, adulthood for fertile people may be caused by reproductive maturity. Fertile people and sterile people possess different physical characteristics and different missions

---

64. Ibid. 68b.
65. *Sanhedrin* pp. 207-209.
66. *Ohr Sameach, Hilchos Sotah* 1:1-2.
67. *Chiddushei Rabbeinu Chaim ha-Levi, Hilchos Ishus* 2:9.

Adulthood

in life[68]; hence, it is logical that they should also possess different parameters of how to reach adulthood.

R. Meir Simcha, as understood by the *Birkas Avraham*,[69] offers a second proof that reproductive maturity does not cause adulthood. A child becomes an adult when two hairs grow on his or her body; witnesses who testify about a single hair are ignored, since we only accept testimony about independently significant fact units.[70] In contrast, a woman suspected of adultery only becomes forbidden to her husband after he warns her not to seclude herself with someone, yet she disobeys and secludes herself with him.[71] We accept witnesses who testify about the warning alone or about the seclusion alone.[72] Why do the warning and the seclusion each count as an independent fact unit, while each hair does not count as an independent unit? After all, warning sans seclusion, like a single hair, has no concrete impact whatsoever! The *Birkas Avraham* answers that hairs do not cause adulthood, they simply indicate that a boy or girl possesses the cognitive characteristics that cause adulthood; hence, they accomplish nothing, neither concrete nor abstract. In contrast, the warning and seclusion each partially cause a woman to become forbidden to her husband; therefore, since each accomplishes

---
68. See *Alei Shur*, vol. 1, pp. 253-254.
69. *Yevamos* pp. 53-54.
70. *Bava Basra* 56b.
71. *Sotah* 2a.
72. Ibid.

something on the abstract level, each is viewed as an independent unit. Even if one agrees that hairs do not cause adulthood, one may challenge the assumption of the *Birkas Avraham* that cognitive factors are the true cause of adulthood. Perhaps hairs indicate that a boy or girl possesses the hormonal or physiological characteristics that comprise reproductive maturity, and those reproductive characteristics are the true cause of adulthood.

R. Soloveitchik,[73] in his analysis of the Rambam's position, distinguishes between childhood's end and adulthood's beginning. Unlike men, who enter adulthood immediately after exiting childhood, women ordinarily endure a transitional phase known as *na'arus*. The laws of *na'arus* differ depending on how *na'arus* is commenced. When *na'arus* is triggered by a girl's growth of two hairs, she loses her childhood privilege of repudiating a marriage that was entered into on her behalf by her mother or brothers. Moreover, when *na'arus* is triggered by two hairs, the *na'arah* immediately begins counting down to adulthood, since she automatically becomes an adult six months after *na'arus* begins. Some laws pertaining to her during this phase contain elements of both childhood and adulthood, while other laws contain elements of neither. For instance, though a child cannot accept marriage tokens on her own behalf and a father cannot accept such tokens on behalf of his adult daughter,

---

73. *Chiddushei Rabbeinu Chaim ha-Levi, Hilchos Ishus* 2:9.

both a *na'arah* and her father may accept marriage tokens on her behalf. Moreover, while a betrothed child (i.e., not yet even a *na'arah*) who was unfaithful to her husband goes unpunished by court, and an unfaithful adult is punished by strangulation, an unfaithful *na'arah* is punished by stoning.

In contrast, writes R. Soloveitchik, *na'arus* triggered by conception of a fetus differs from *na'arus* triggered by two hairs. Although a girl who conceives, like an ordinary *na'arah*, loses her childhood privilege of repudiating a marriage contracted on her behalf by her mother or brothers and begins counting down to adulthood, she remains a child in all other respects. This means, for instance, that she may not accept marriage tokens on her own behalf. Only after reaching age twelve, and after delivering a healthy baby, does she transition into full adulthood.

Just as adulthood is determined partially by age, so that any girl under twelve years of age is a child, and is therefore not punished by court for her sins, suitability for *bi'ah* is also determined by age, and any girl under three years of age or any boy under nine cannot, through intercourse, achieve any of the following: enter a marriage or *yibbum* relationship; transmit or receive the ritual impurity of menstruant women; disqualify herself from eating *terumah*; and render his or her partner liable to capital punishment.[74] And, just as we inquired about to what extent the ages of twelve

---

74. *Yevamos* 57b.

and thirteen correspond to reproductive milestones, we must inquire to what extent the ages of three and nine correspond to reproductive milestones.

Beis Shammai[75] discuss the following calamitous possibility: what is the *halakhah* if an eight-year-old boy had intercourse with a close relative? Does he disqualify his partner from subsequently marrying a *kohein* (priest), or not? Beis Shammai conclude that he absolutely does disqualify his partner. Similarly, Rashi[76] maintains that an infant under three years of age who engaged in intercourse with a gentile becomes disqualified to marry a *kohein*. Moreover, the Rashba[77] entertains the possibility that intercourse with a girl under three can be halakhically considered *bi'ah* in almost every way (though he concludes otherwise). These sources indicate that *bi'ah*, in some contexts, does not correspond to reproductive maturity.

However, the overwhelming majority of authoritative sources indicate the opposite, that the road to *bi'ah* is marked with reproductive milestones. Hence, the Rashba[78] concludes that intercourse with a girl under three is in no way treated as *bi'ah*. Rashi[79] explains that in some way, the *dam besulim* (hymeneal ring) regenerates in girls under three, and only remains permanently broken in girls over three. Since the

---

75. *Sanhedrin* 69b.
76. *Yevamos* 60b.
77. *Yevamos* 57b.
78. Ibid.
79. *Sanhedrin* 55b.

Talmud[80] believes that *dam besulim* prevents a woman from becoming pregnant, it is logical to suggest that age three is significant because at that age, a woman's body will no longer reverse itself from a state that renders it more suitable for reproduction.

Similarly, the Talmud[81] writes explicitly that after age nine, men can produce seed, and therefore, after age nine, a boy's intercourse is halakhically treated as *bi'ah*.

---

80. *Yevamos* 34a.
81. *Sanhedrin* 69a.

Chapter 4

Marriage

Marriage, as an ethical imperative and a legal institution, possesses many overlapping themes. Traditional sources associate marriage with procreation[82]; avoidance of forbidden thoughts or relationships[83]; optimal child-rearing[84]; provenance and receipt of pleasure,[85] security, and dignity; and creating an abode for Hashem's presence. The laws of marriage echo each of these themes. This chapter will analyze the extent to which these themes, and particularly the theme of procreation, shape the contours of marriage law.

At first glance, marriage and procreation share little common ground. One can fulfill procreation without marrying, and one can marry without procreating. Indeed, the Rosh[86] believes that marriage is neither an independent mitzvah nor a prerequisite for *peru u-revu*. Hence, the blessing recited at marriage is not a *birkas ha-mitzvah*, a blessing recited over a mitzvah, which may

---

82. *Tur, Even ha-Ezer* 1.
83. *Yevamos* 63b, *Sefer ha-Chinnuch* 582.
84. *Yevamos* 63a.
85. R. Joseph Dov Soloveitchik, *Family Redeemed*, pp. 50-52.
86. *Kesubos* 1:12.

only be recited before the mitzvah is performed. Rather, the blessing recited at marriage is a *birkas ha-shevach*, a blessing of praise to Hashem for an extraordinary experience, and hence may be recited even after the experience.

Similarly, although the Talmud[87] exempts women from procreation, the Talmud seems to obligate women in marriage. The Talmud[88] writes that women should not appoint agents to accept marriage tokens on their behalf, since women have a mitzvah to marry, and the mitzvah is greater when performed personally than when performed by an agent. Some Rishonim[89] even rule that a woman who accepted her marriage token through an agent should, when the opportunity arises, accept anew a marriage token in person. In addition, R. Dan Ashkenazi[90] and R. Nissim of Gerona[91] permit women to annul oaths against marriage, since such annulment facilitates their performance of the marriage mitzvah.

Many Rishonim, however, reinterpret the talmudic passages that obligate women in marriage and exempt them from procreation. These Rishonim are motivated by their conviction that marriage and procreation are inextricably intertwined, and women must be either equally obligated or equally exempt from both. R.

---

87. *Yevamos* 65b.
88. *Kiddushin* 42a.
89. See *Shut ha-Rivash* 82.
90. Cited in *Shut ha-Ran* 32, and *Shut ha-Rashba ha-Meyuchasos le-Ramban* 250.
91. *Shut ha-Ran* 27, 32, 53, and 55.

Dan Ashkenazi[92] writes that women are not bound to procreate and therefore not bound to marry; when the Talmud says they have a mitzvah to marry, it means that their performance of procreation or their entrance into marriage is considered meritorious. In talmudic language, they receive the merit of *eino metzuveh ve-oseh*, one who fulfills a mitzvah even though he or she is not commanded to do so. The Ritva[93] claims that women as a collective are obligated to procreate and marry; when the Talmud writes that women are exempt from procreation, it means that individual women are exempt from both marriage and procreation. Finally, R. Nissim[94] writes that women are obligated to marry in order to help men fulfill their mitzvah of *peru u-revu*; however, they are not obligated themselves to fulfill that mitzvah. Finally, without addressing the talmudic passage that seems to obligate women to marry, the Rashba[95] claims that since women are not bound to procreate, they cannot be bound to marry.

By associating marriage with *peru u-revu*, these authorities follow the opinion of R. Achai Gaon's *She'iltos*,[96] that one who had children outside of marriage did not fully fulfill his mitzvah, and should therefore, for full fulfillment, marry and sire children with his wife. This opinion is based on the verse, "take

---

92. Cited in *Shut ha-Ran* 32, and *Shut ha-Rashba ha-Meyuchasos le-Ramban* 250.
93. *Shut ha-Ritva* 43.
94. *Shut ha-Ran* 27, 32, 53, and 55.
95. *Shut ha-Rashba* 1:602.
96. *She'ilta* 165.

wives and have sons and daughters." The Netziv[97] notes that, counterintuitively, the scope of *peru u-revu* diminishes on account of its association with marriage. Whereas an independent mitzvah of *peru u-revu* would obligate a man to engage in intercourse when possible on a nightly basis, Rambam[98] writes that *peru u-revu* as attenuated by marriage only obligates him to engage in intercourse on the nights implicitly agreed upon at the time of marriage. One may further note that one man may marry many women, perhaps since one man can father children through each wife, while one woman may only marry one man, perhaps since a woman can only bear children to one man at a time.[99] Finally, the *Shut Lev Avraham*[100] writes that women may not take contraceptive measures without permission from their husbands, since the purpose of marriage is procreation, and therefore every woman who consents to marriage *ipso facto* obligates herself to assist her husband in fulfilling his mitzvah.

While the Netziv integrates the marriage mitzvah and *peru u-revu* within the Rambam's perspective, my rebbe, R. Michael Rosensweig,[101] argues that the

---

97. *Ha'amek She'elah* to *She'ilta* 165, no. 1 (vol. 3, pp. 276-277).
98. *Hilchos Ishus* 15:1.
99. See *Kiddushin* 7a.
100. No. 99.
101. "*Be-Inyan Shitas ha-Rambam be-Kesubah de-Oraisa o de-Rabanan*," *Beis Yitzchak* 26, pp. 441-450; "*Be-Inyan Shitas ha-Rambam be-Mitzvas Kiddushin*," *Hazon Nahum* (Hebrew section) pp. 35-45; "*Shitas ha-Rambam be-Inyan Kedeishah u-Pilegesh u-Mitzvas Kiddushin*," *Beis Yitzchak* 38, pp. 107-114.

Rambam's conception of the mitzvah of marriage extends far beyond *peru u-revu*. The mitzvah of marriage is designed to provide women with dignity and security, so that they are not merely objects *through* whom to fulfill *peru u-revu*, but subjects *with* whom to build a sacred relationship. Hence, the Rambam[102] writes that one who marries a woman in an undignified setting is liable to lashes, as is one who marries a woman without first proposing to her,[103] and one who creates marriage via an intimate act of intercourse without first achieving platonic familiarity.[104] Such marriages conform to the letter of the law, but defy its spirit. Moreover, one who marries a woman without signing the *kesubah* contract—designed to discourage divorce, to make the woman feel that her marriage is secure, and to protect the woman's financial security in the event of divorce or death—does not fulfill his mitzvah of marriage.[105] Indeed, one may not proceed to intercourse unless he has given his wife her *kesubah*.[106] Furthermore, while *halakhah* acknowledges stipulations that limit monetary obligations, it does not acknowledge such stipulations when they pertain to a *kesubah*.[107] Stipulations of the *kesubah* are security-related, mitzvah-related, and not merely money-related.

---

102. *Hilchos Ishus* 3:21-22.
103. Ibid.
104. Ibid.
105. Rambam *Koteres* to *Hilchos Ishus*.
106. Rambam *Hilchos Ishus* 10:7.
107. Rambam *Hilchos Ishus* 10:9, 12:6-8.

Along similar lines, R. Nissim[108] notes that one only completely fulfills the mitzvah of marriage with the partner he or she desires to marry. Hence, we may annul vows to allow a man and woman who desire to marry each other, since such annulment is necessary for the mitzvah's fulfillment, even though the man and woman could each marry a different spouse and fulfill *peru u-revu* without violating their oath. Similarly, R. Nissim[109] claims that Chazal[110] forbade us to marry off minors because a child cannot maturely determine whom she desires to marry.

Interestingly, while imbuing marriage with dignity, security, and love is an inherently worthwhile project, the *Iggeres ha-Kodesh* (an early medieval work attributed to the Ramban)[111] relates it to *peru u-revu*:

> It is fitting for him to settle his wife's mind, to make her happy, to prepare her, and to draw her with things that gladden the heart, so that she should agree to pure and beautiful thoughts, so the two of them will unite in the mitzvah [of procreation], since then their thoughts will be as one and Hashem's presence will unfold in their midst, *and they will give birth to a son [whose qualities] reflect the pure form that they formed.*

---

108. *Shut ha-Ran* 27, 32, 53, and 55.
109. Ibid.
110. *Kiddushin* 42a.
111. Ch. 5.

The Ramban mentioned "Hashem's presence unfolding in their midst." For R. Shlomo Wolbe,[112] this may be the main theme of marriage. Why, asks R. Wolbe, are we commanded to gladden a groom and bride? Because, he answers, Hashem's presence only unfolds in a joyous setting. R. Wolbe cites abundant aggadic evidence for his thesis, but little halakhic evidence. Nonetheless, piquantly, the purpose R. Wolbe ascribes to marriage has been equally ascribed to *peru u-revu*.

R. Yaakov[113] opines that one who neglects *peru u-revu* "diminishes the likeness [of Hashem in this world]." The *Kedushas Levi* explains that each individual reflects a unique facet of the divine likeness, just as each student of a teacher might adopt a unique characteristic of that teacher's methodology or style. Hence R. Huna[114] claims that one whose children died still fulfills the mitzvah of *peru u-revu*, since he helped, however briefly, to reflect in this world a unique facet of the divine likeness. Although *halakhah* rejects R. Huna's opinion, and one whose children died must father more children, we nevertheless see the degree to which both marriage and procreation contribute to unfolding the divine presence in this world.

---

112. *Alei Shur*, vol. 1, pp. 255-258.
113. *Yevamos* 63b.
114. *Yevamos* 62a.

Chapter 5

Intercourse

What is the purpose of intercourse? The *Tur*[115] writes that during intercourse men should be mindful of four intentions and should avoid a fifth intention. First, one should intend to produce children. The Raavad[116] writes that this is the most meritorious intention one can have during intercourse. Second, one should intend to give pleasure to his wife. Third, one should intend to increase his love and desire for his wife, to render himself less vulnerable to sirens. Fourth, he should intend to maintain his health by keeping equilibrium amongst his humors. The *Tur* adds that men should *not* engage in intercourse solely for their own pleasure.

To what extent are these five intentions reflected in halakhic definitions of intercourse (*bi'ah*)? Does *halakhah* define intercourse that cannot result in children as *bi'ah*, or not? Does it define as *bi'ah* intercourse that can result in children but cannot fulfill the other purposes of intercourse, or not?

Intercourse that does not or cannot result in children is deemed deficient in a number of halakhic

---
115. *Tur, Orach Chaim* 240.
116. Cited in *Tur*, ibid.

contexts. Most notably, there are three opinions about precisely how *mitzvas peru u-revu* is fulfilled. The *Minchas Chinnuch*[117] holds that one only fulfills *peru u-revu* by attaining children, and one does not fulfill the mitzvah by engaging in intercourse. For this reason, someone whose children died must still fulfill the mitzvah, while someone who became obligated in *peru u-revu* after his children were born is considered to have completely fulfilled the mitzvah.[118] Moreover, someone who impregnated his wife without physical contact (e.g., via artificial insemination) fully fulfills his mitzvah.[119] In contrast, R. Tzvi Pesach Frank[120] argues that the Torah cannot command us to attain children; such a command would be inherently unfair, since conception and healthy delivery are beyond human control. Rather, one fulfills *peru u-revu* simply by engaging in intercourse that can result in pregnancy. For this reason, one who conceives a child in sin does not fulfill *peru u-revu* according to the Rambam,[121] since the intercourse's sinful character precludes it from serving to fulfill the mitzvah. (In talmudic language, this concept is known as *mitzvah ha-ba'ah ba-aveirah*. If a single action is at once a mitzvah and an *aveirah* (a sin), its *aveirah* dimension precludes it from counting as a mitzvah. Hence, a sinful *bi'ah* cannot count as fulfilling the *mitzvah* of *peru u-revu*.) Yet

---

117. Mitzvah 1.
118. *Yevamos* 62a.
119. See *Chelkas Mechokek, Even ha-Ezer* 1:8.
120. *Shut Har Tzvi, Orach Chaim* 2:76.
121. See *Aruch la-Ner* to *Yevamos* 22a.

R. Frank and the Rambam must agree that one whose children died has yet to fulfill the mitzvah, perhaps because intercourse that does not produce surviving offspring is deficient and does not completely fulfill the mitzvah.

An astonishing and resoundingly rejected parallel is cited by R. Avraham ibn Ezra[122]: adulterous intercourse that does not result in conception cannot render its participants liable to capital punishment. Chazal, however, derive that adulterers are liable even for incomplete intercourse or *bi'ah shelo ke-darkah*,[123] so *peru u-revu* remains the only area of *halakhah* where intercourse that does not produce children does not satisfy the halakhic requirement for *bi'ah*.

Two further areas of *halakhah* emphasize the procreative dimension of intercourse. R. Nissim Gaon and Rabbeinu Nesanel[124] write that *kiddushin*, the initial stage of marriage, when contracted through intercourse, can only be generated by complete intercourse (*bi'ah gemurah*). Hence, in the strange and distressing theoretical circumstance of a woman who, in the midst of contracting *kiddushin* with one man via intercourse, accepted a wedding ring from a different man, *halakhah* considers her married to the ring-giver rather than to her partner in intercourse.

---

122. *Vayikra* 18:20.
123. *Yevamos* 55b.
124. Cited, respectively, in *Tosafos R. Peretz* and *Tosafos Yeshanim* to *Yevamos*, ibid.

Similarly, Tosafos[125] maintain that ideally, the mitzvah of *yibbum* (levirate marriage) can only be fulfilled via intercourse that can result in conception; for technical reasons, however, Tosafos hold that even partial intercourse, which is unsuitable for conception, can both satisfy the mitzvah of *yibbum* and grant the participants in *yibbum* full status as a married couple. Still, the ideal requirement of intercourse that can result in conception is reflected through the law that intercourse without an erection does not fulfill the mitzvah of *yibbum*. In contrast, the Rashba[126] rules that *mitzvas yibbum* is not fulfilled until the man produces seed, although intercourse without seed still grants its participants status as a married couple. The Talmud Yerushalmi, as interpreted by Tosafos,[127] extends this idea even further, and withholds from the couple some privileges unique to marriage until a complete intercourse, with seed, is performed. Hence, a *kohein's yevamah* (widow of a deceased, childless brother) may not partake of *terumah* until she performs *yibbum* via a complete intercourse, and the *kohein* may not annul her vows, inherit her, or bury her unless he previously acquired her via complete intercourse.

Moreover, R. Menachem ha-Meiri[128] writes that one cannot fulfill *mitzvas yibbum* via his first intercourse with a *besulah* (virgin), since such intercourse often does

---

125. *Yevamos* 53b.
126. *Yevamos* 20b.
127. *Yevamos* 56a.
128. *Yevamos* 20a.

not result in pregnancy. This results in the following leniency. A *kohein gadol* ordinarily may not marry a widow. However, the Torah makes an exception to this requirement when the marriage will be created via *yibbum*, and permits the *kohein gadol* to have intercourse with a widow for as long as it takes to fulfill his mitzvah. Most Rishonim understand that the mitzvah is fulfilled via the first intercourse or the first moments of intercourse. However, the Meiri suggests that when the widow is a *besulah*, who cannot become pregnant until she has intercourse twice, the *kohein gadol* may biblically engage in two acts of intercourse. Since both acts of intercourse are necessary to make her pregnant, both fulfill *mitzvas yibbum*, and both override the widow prohibition. Only subsequent acts of intercourse, which do not contribute to the mitzvah's fulfillment, must be foregone on account of the widow prohibition.

These proofs from *kiddushin* and *yibbum* are somewhat flawed, since men or women incapable of conceiving children are not necessarily barred from generating *kiddushin* or *yibbum* via intercourse. This is probably due to the necessity for maintaining a uniform definition of *bi'ah* in different areas of *halakhah*. *Halakhah*'s circumscription of the efficacy of intercourse not suited for conception to create *kiddushin*, fulfill *mitzvas yibbum*, and grant the *yavam* and *yevamah* privileges probably symbolizes that procreation is an integral element of *bi'ah* in the contexts of *kiddushin* and *yibbum*.

The Torah, in a few other contexts, also insists on intercourse suitable for conception. For instance, one who violates a *shifchah charufah* (a gentile slave betrothed to a Jewish slave) may only bring an atonement sacrifice if he violated her via intercourse suitable for conception.[129] Presumably, the sacrifice atones for his possibility of producing children with her, not for his pleasure or his establishing an intimate relationship with her. Similarly, a *kohein* who has intercourse with a divorcee or a promiscuous woman is only liable for complete intercourse, since the Torah was primarily concerned lest he father a child with her.[130] Moreover, the *Minchas Chinnuch*[131] writes that one only violates the prohibition of "*lo tihyeh kedeishah*," which prohibits intercourse with an unmarried woman, if his intercourse was suitable to impregnate her. Since the Torah's concern was to curb proliferation of such unions' children, lest they come to inadvertently marry their half-siblings, only intercourse that can produce children is punishable.

Finally, the Talmud[132] rules that partial intercourse, *bi'ah shelo ke-darkah*, and perhaps even intercourse with a *besulah*, even when accompanied by emission of seed, do not transmit the ritual impurity ordinarily conveyed by emission of seed. This is because such acts of intercourse cannot result in children.

---

129. *Yevamos* 55a.
130. *Kiddushin* 78a.
131. Mitzvah 570.
132. *Yevamos* 34b.

It is interesting to note that R. Yehudah opines that intercourse without *pirtzah*, facilitating the expansion of human civilization, is considered promiscuous (*bi'as zenus*).[133] Therefore, R. Yehudah rules that a *kohein*, who may not marry a promiscuous woman, may not marry a sterile woman. Although *halakhah* rejects R. Yehudah's opinion, the Talmud[134] mentions that King David would abstain from intercourse with his wives when they were pregnant, presumably because such intercourse would not facilitate the expansion of human civilization. Yet King David's practice also is not halakhically normative; men must engage in intercourse with their wives even when they are incapable of conceiving, to provide them with pleasure and to strengthen their love for them.

What role does pleasure play in the halakhic definition of intercourse? The Talmud[135] writes that one who performs ordinary sins with inadequate levels of intentionality (*mis'asek*) is exempt from punishment, yet one who unintentionally engages in forbidden intercourse is not exempt, because forbidden intercourse is pleasurable. This may indicate that one has a higher level of responsibility to premeditatedly avoid pleasant sins, or that the pleasure restores what the lack of intention damaged, namely, the connection between the action and actor. R. Naftali Gettinger,[136] however,

---

133. *Yevamos* 61b.
134. *Sanhedrin* 70b.
135. *Kerisos* 19b.
136. Cited in R. Yosef Radner, *Nachalas Mayim*, p. 98.

makes a more ambitious argument. Perhaps sinners who do not derive pleasure are punished for their actions, while sinners who derive pleasure are punished for the pleasure itself. R. Gettinger's thesis indicates that the most salient characteristic of forbidden intercourse is the pleasure it provides.

The laws of *hotza'as zera le-vatalah* may also emphasize pleasure's role in intercourse. Some authorities maintain that the verse *lo sin'af*, "do not be adulterous," teaches us the prohibition against *hotza'as zera le-vatalah*. Indeed, the *Shut Yaskil Avdi*[137] writes that just as one must sacrifice his life rather than commit adultery, one must give up his life rather than perform *hotza'as zera le-vatalah*. This opinion, however, is roundly rejected by the consensus of rabbinic authorities. *Hotza'as zera le-vatalah* does not carry the death penalty, and one must not sacrifice his life to avoid it. Indeed, people who have difficulty controlling their *hotza'as zera* sometimes spiral into deeper and deeper depression over what they perceive as unforgivable transgressions. Such surrender to depression is exactly the opposite of what Hashem wants them to do. Rather than become depressed, these people should consult psychologically sensitive spiritual mentors, such as their community rabbi or the *mashgiach* of their yeshiva, to construct an effective and permissible plan of action to combat their difficulty.

Returning to our topic, we ask: what does *hotza'as zera le-vatalah* have in common with adultery? Although

---

137. Cited in *Otzar ha-Poskim*, vol. 9, p. 177.

one may argue that *hotza'as zera le-vatalah* and adultery both provoke Hashem's anger (*af*), or that both involve diversion of energy from positive channels to wasteful or destructive ones, one may also argue that the common denominator of adultery and *hotza'as zera le-vatalah* is non-wife-centered experience of intimate pleasure. Based on this, some authorities forbid *hotza'as zera le-vatalah* for semen analysis, because it is a non-wife-centered intimately pleasant experience.[138] As an aside, having mentioned the topic of semen analysis, we advise the reader that many rabbis permit *hotza'as zera* for such analysis, based on a variety of reasons. Not every circumstance, however, provides sufficient grounds for permission. Every person should therefore consult his rabbi if his doctor recommends that he undergo such analysis.

Although procreation and pleasure both contribute to the halakhic definition of *bi'ah*, the most important characteristic of *bi'ah* is creation or reinforcement of an intimate relationship. For this reason, even partial intercourse or *bi'ah shelo ke-darkah*, which cannot result in conception, are defined as *bi'ah*. Indeed, the Talmud[139] even contemplates defining as *bi'ah* the lightest imaginable contact between male and female reproductive organs. Such contact will not result in conception, nor will it afford more pleasure than contact between the male organ and some less

---

138. For more on this topic, see Chapter 7 of this book.
139. *Yevamos* 55b.

private part of the female's body. This contact is only significant inasmuch as it represents the woman's consent to bare her womb, to surrender stewardship of her reproductive powers to a man, or in other words, inasmuch as it creates an intimate relationship between woman and man. R. Nissim Karelitz[140] interprets even the Talmud's conclusion—that light contact does not constitute *bi'ah*, and partial penetration is necessary—not as associating *bi'ah* with the higher level of pleasure attained by penetration, but rather as associating *bi'ah* with creation of deep intimate relationships.

For the same reason, *nissu'in*, the final stage of halakhic marriage, may be created via intercourse or via *chuppah*.[141] *Chuppah* and intercourse share a common denominator, namely, the woman's consent to grant a man intimacy rights and stewardship over her reproductive capacity, even though *chuppah* is more formal and symbolic while intercourse is less formal.

Similarly, the Rambam[142] maintains that one must sacrifice his life rather than kiss or hug a forbidden woman (i.e., a woman married to someone else, or a *niddah*), just as one must sacrifice his life rather than have intercourse with her. The common denominator shared by kissing and intercourse is creation of intimacy.

Further support for this idea can be adduced from the law that intercourse with an animal differs

---

140. *Chut Shani, Yoreh Deah* 192, fn. 30.
141. See *Shulchan Aruch, Even ha-Ezer* 61.
142. *Hilchos Issurei Bi'ah* 21:1, as interpreted by *Beis Yosef, Yoreh Deah* 195.

fundamentally from intercourse with a human. While one may sacrifice in the temple a lamb exchanged for permission to have intercourse with an animal (*esnan kelev*), one may not sacrifice a lamb exchanged for permission to have intercourse with a woman (*esnan zonah*).[143] Although both types of intercourse provide equal pleasure, only intercourse with a human creates intimate relationships; intercourse with an animal, with a different, non-sentient species, cannot create intimacy.

Thus far, we have analyzed the respective roles played in defining *bi'ah* by procreation, pleasure, and building relationships. We have seen that regarding *peru u-revu*, *kiddushin*, and *yibbum*, the *halakhah* places greater emphasis on the importance of procreation to *bi'ah*, while regarding *nissu'in* and forbidden women, *halakhah* places greater emphasis on pleasure or on relationships. Still other areas of *halakhah* contain controversies over which dimension of intercourse to emphasize. For instance, a groom may not seclude himself with his wife if she is a menstruant unless they have already had intercourse before she became a *niddah*. If they did not successfully engage in first intercourse, we are concerned that his *yetzer hara*, his passional evil inclination, will convince him to have intercourse with her in violation of the *niddah* prohibition. R. Shmuel Wosner[144] holds that successful first intercourse means

---

143. *Yevamos* 59b.
144. *Shiurei Shevet ha-Levi* to *Yoreh Deah* 192:4.

complete intercourse. In contrast, R. Nissim Karelitz[145] argues that even a partial intercourse pacifies the *yetzer hara*. R. Dovid Feinstein[146] advances a third opinion, that even minimal contact or less between the male and female organs pacifies the *yetzer hara*.

---

145. *Chut Shani*, ibid.
146. Cited by Rabbi Baruch Simon in a personal communication.

Chapter 6

Sirus

The Torah[147] forbids us to intentionally, mechanically sterilize male humans or animals (*sirus*). Many authorities forbid even: unintentional *sirus*, such as when *sirus* is the side effect of a healing potion or procedure; *sirus* of females, such as by hysterectomy; chemical sterilization; and *sirus* of fish. Yet other authorities permit these types of *sirus*, at least on a biblical level. Obviously, in situations where we permit *sirus*, we still require its subject's consent, and we also require the act of *sirus* to serve a constructive purpose. It is difficult to properly analyze the topic of *sirus*, due to the dearth of unambiguous primary sources. Nevertheless, this chapter will explicate four potential conceptual bases for the *sirus* prohibition, and the unique halakhic framework that fits each basis.

The *Sefer ha-Chinnuch*[148] writes that *sirus* is forbidden because it diminishes the reproductive capacity of a species and leads that species towards extinction. Based on this, the *Minchas Chinnuch*[149] suggests that *sirus*

---
147. *Vayikra* 22:24.
148. Mitzvah 291.
149. Ibid.

of women and of fish should be forbidden, as should be indirect *sirus* and *sirus* by chemical means. Moreover, we should be forbidden to inhibit reproduction even without interfering with the reproductive system, such as by means of condoms or of hypnosis. After all, each of these actions diminishes the reproductive capacity of its subject's species. Finally, we should be permitted to perform *sirus* on sterile creatures, since such *sirus* does not bring a species closer to extinction. Indeed, the Talmud[150] seems to clearly permit *sirus* of old men, if we could determine with certainty that they had already lost their fertility and that no medication or procedure could restore their fertility. However, not all the other suppositions are halakhically true. Everyone agrees that sterilization by hypnosis is permitted, as is locking a female animal's reproductive organs with a ring to prevent it from engaging in intercourse.[151]

Along similar lines as the *Sefer ha-Chinnuch*, the *Mabit*[152] writes that *sirus* is forbidden because it forces its subjects to neglect the mitzvah of *peru u-revu*. Based on this, the *Mabit* permits *sirus* of women, since women are not commanded in *peru u-revu*. However, this position is difficult to comprehend, since everyone forbids *sirus* of animals, even though animals are not commanded in *peru u-revu*.[153] Moreover, everyone

---

150. *Shabbos* 111a.
151. *Shabbos* 54a, 110b.
152. *Kriyas Sefer, Hilchos Issurei Bi'ah* 16:12.
153. *Even ha-Ezer* 5:11.

agrees that one may not perform *sirus* after *sirus*,[154] even though the latter act of *sirus* has no further impact on its subject's ability to fulfill *peru u-revu*.

While the *Sefer ha-Chinnuch* and the *Mabit* focus on the result of *sirus*, the *Taz*[155] focuses on the action of *sirus* itself. *Sirus* is forbidden, claims the *Taz*, because it wounds and pains its subjects. Based on this, one may perform *sirus* on an animal to save it from death, since death is far worse than injury or pain.[156] Moreover, one may perform *sirus* through chemical means, if the chemicals cause no physical wounds or pain. Furthermore, just as we do not biblically punish people who damage property or wound others indirectly (*grama*), we would not punish those who neuter animals indirectly, such as by holding them underwater until their reproductive organs freeze.[157] However, the *Taz* does not explain why one may perform *sirus* on infertile elders.

Perhaps the most compelling explanation for why *sirus* is forbidden is hinted at by the *Sefer ha-Chinnuch*.[158] When one sterilizes a creature, he symbolically indicates that "he is disgusted with the Creator's handiwork, and he desires the destruction of His good world." Castration and similar actions symbolically demonstrate, and powerfully so, one's opposition to reproduction and to proliferation of life. For this

---

154. *Shabbos* 111a.
155. *Even ha-Ezer* 5:6.
156. See *Pischei Teshuvah, Even ha-Ezer* 5:10.
157. *Even ha-Ezer* 5:13.
158. Mitzvah 291.

reason, one may perform *sirus* if he limits or distorts its negative symbolic quality. Hence, the Torah does not forbid ingesting medicinal potions whose side effects leave one sterile, such as chemotherapy for cancer patients, because the act's medicinal context mutes its anti-reproductive symbolism. Similarly, we do not punish people who perform sterilization indirectly (*grama*), such as through a potion, or by inciting an animal to attack the reproductive organs.[159] The Torah only punishes direct contact with the reproductive organs, since only such contact can fully symbolically convey one's disgust with reproduction. Moreover, some authorities claim that one may sterilize women because their reproductive organs are concealed, just as we may sacrifice animals with deformities in their concealed organs.[160] The basis for this ruling may be that the symbolic force of a hysterectomy is much muted, since the procedure leaves no revealed evidence of having taken place.

This approach dovetails with the Rashba's solution to an otherwise intractable contradiction. The Talmud[161] permits *sirus* of an infertile elder, indicating that we are only forbidden to sterilize an otherwise fertile creature. Yet the Talmud[162] forbids castration of previously sterilized creatures, indicating that we are forbidden to perform a destructive action on the

---

159. *Even ha-Ezer* 5:12-13.
160. See *Taz*, ibid.
161. *Shabbos* 111a.
162. Ibid.

reproductive organs, whether or not they are functional. How do infertile elders differ from otherwise sterile creatures? The Rashba[163] responds that to the uninformed onlooker, elders appear incapable of reproduction, since everyone knows that reproductive capacity dwindles with age, while to the uninformed onlooker, sterile people may still appear fertile. Hence, *sirus* of a sterile creature, although physiologically inconsequential, is forbidden since it still has intense symbolic significance to the uninformed onlooker, while *sirus* of an infertile elder is permitted since its negative symbolic content is low.

---

163. Ibid.

Chapter 7

Hotza'as Zera le-Vatalah

The Talmud[164] rules that men are enjoined from destroying or devaluing their seed. In Talmudic language, this is called *hashchasas zera*, destroying seed, or *hotza'as zera le-vatalah*, devaluing emission of seed. Although this prohibition is never explicitly articulated by the Torah, the Zohar[165] treats it in some ways as the most stringent of all sins, and writes that repentance cannot expiate its punishment. Hence, some authorities treat the prohibition as spiritual, metaphysical, and beyond the realm of human comprehension. Therefore, these authorities claim that halakhic teleology cannot help us determine the prohibition's parameters; rather, tradition alone can determine those parameters, and when tradition is absent, we must be stringent. However, other authorities are more favorably disposed to clarifying the prohibition's parameters via teleological induction and deduction. Even so, these authorities differ as to the prohibition's precise purpose. This chapter will survey some theoretical bases of *hotza'as zera le-vatalah* and their impact on the prohibition's parameters.

---

164. *Yevamos* 34b.
165. Cited by *Beis Yosef, Even ha-Ezer* 23.

The *Levush*[166] writes that *hotza'as zera le-vatalah* is forbidden because it decreases reproduction. Along similar lines, the Tosafos[167] imply that destroying seed is forbidden because it violates the *mitzvah* of *peru u-revu*. For this reason, women and gentiles, who have no *mitzvah* of *peru u-revu*, are permitted to destroy seed. Similarly, Rambam[168] writes that one should not marry a young girl, since intercourse with her cannot result in children and is therefore similar to *hotza'as zera le-vatalah*. Moreover, the *Beis Yitzchak*[169] writes that one who already fulfilled *peru u-revu* is biblically permitted to destroy his seed, and only rabbinically forbidden from doing so. Furthermore, the *Minchas Chinnuch*[170] entertains the possibility that a eunuch may destroy his seed, since that seed is incapable of developing into a child. Many authorities[171] cite these positions as precedent to permit infertile couples to emit seed for semen analysis or in vitro fertilization (IVF); since the seed would anyhow not result in offspring, emitting it does not further violate *peru u-revu*.

However, R. Shlomo Zalman Auerbach[172] critiques these positions, claiming that if they were true, then even a man traveling away from his wife or the husband of a sterile woman would be permitted to emit seed,

---

166. *Even ha-Ezer* 23.
167. *Yevamos* 12b.
168. *Hilchos Issurei Bi'ah* 21:18.
169. Cited by *Otzar ha-Poskim*, vol. 9, p. 165.
170. Mitzvah 1.
171. See *Otzar ha-Poskim* ibid. p. 166.
172. Cited by *Nishmas Avraham, Even ha-Ezer* 23:1.

since their seed would anyhow not result in offspring. Similarly, the *Shut Rav Pe'alim*[173] writes that if these positions were true, one would be forbidden to have intercourse with his pregnant wife, since seed from such intercourse would not result in children. Hence, some other theoretical basis for forbidding *hotza'as zera le-vatalah* must be found.

Such a basis may emerge from analysis of a contradiction posed by Tosafos. The Talmud[174] writes that we may not destroy seed, yet the Talmud[175] permits us to engage in *bi'ah shelo ke-darkah*, even though such intercourse will result in *hotza'as zera*. Tosafos respond that one may not devalue his seed on a constant basis, since this course of action will addict him to purposeless pleasure and enslave him to his evil inclination. However, one may on rare occasions engage in intercourse wherein seed is devalued. Hence, the *Divrei Ta'am*[176] forbids even sterile men, and certainly men who are traveling away from their wives or whose wives are sterile, from emitting seed for pleasure, lest they become slaves to pleasure. Conversely, however, the *Beis Shmuel*[177] writes that potentially infertile men— who would be biblically forbidden from marrying ancestral Jews on account of their infertility—may emit seed to test their fertility. Although other authorities

---

173. Cited by *Otzar ha-Poskim*, ibid. pp. 165-166.
174. *Yevamos* 34b.
175. *Nedarim* 20b, *Sanhedrin* 59b.
176. Cited in *Otzar ha-Poskim*, ibid.
177. *Even ha-Ezer* 25:2, based on *Yevamos* 76a.

suggest various reasons to permit this fertility test, the *Beis Shmuel* claims that it is permitted because it will not addict anyone to purposeless pleasure. Based on this, one can beautifully explain the *Shulchan Aruch*'s[178] prohibition against reading romance novels and books on marital arts. While most commentaries explain that these texts are forbidden because they lead to emission of seed, Tosafos can explain that they are forbidden for the selfsame reason as emission of seed: to prevent people from becoming slaves to pleasure.

The *Piskei Rid*[179] suggests an alternate resolution to the Tosafos' contradiction: one may not destroy seed with bad intentions, such as with intention to prevent conception to preserve one's wife's figure, but one may destroy seed with good intentions, such as intention to make one's wife happy or to "make his evil inclination's passion less belligerent" (*le-hashlim ta'avas yitzro*). For this reason, the *Sefer Chasidim*[180] permits people to emit seed if they fear that otherwise they might commit adultery or have intercourse with a menstruant woman. This indicates that Hashem wants us to harmonize our desire with His will, and forbids *hotza'as zera le-vatalah* when such conduct stems from and contributes to the divergence of our will from His will.

According to these resolutions of Tosafos' contradiction, one should be permitted to emit seed for semen analysis or IVF, since such emissions only occur

---

178. *Orach Chaim* 307:16.
179. *Yevamos* 12b.
180. Cited by *Beis Shmuel, Even ha-Ezer* 23:1.

on rare occasions and with good intentions. However, Tosafos[181] offer a third resolution that potentially forbids semen analysis and IVF. Perhaps, suggest Tosafos, *bi'ah shelo ke-darkah* is permitted only when unaccompanied by seminal emission, and otherwise is forbidden. The *Aruch ha-Shulchan*[182] explains that Hashem imbued men with desire for intercourse to encourage perpetuation of the human species. Nature itself proves this teleology of pleasure. As soon as seed leaves the body, man's pleasure ceases; the pleasure disappears once it fulfills its purpose, once the act of species perpetuation was performed. Similarly, old or infirm men who can no longer reproduce desire women less, since such desire would not contribute to the species' perpetuation. We learn from nature that pleasure is only legitimate when it leads directly to children; when the pleasure connects only indirectly to children, and certainly when the pleasure connects not at all to children, it is illegitimate. Since so many things can prevent seed emitted for semen analysis or IVF from resulting in children, and since for millennia emissions without intercourse could not help produce children, such acts of emission are disconnected from children and therefore deemed potentially illegitimate.[183] Once again, however, the reader is reminded that many grounds exist for permitting semen analysis, and certainly for IVF, and if his doctor recommends either of these procedures, he should ask his rabbi how to proceed.

---

181. *Yevamos* 34b.
182. *Even ha-Ezer* 23:1.
183. See *Otzar ha-Poskim*, ibid. p. 177.

Based on this, however, we can understand why the authorities who forbid emission of seed for semen analysis or IVF nevertheless permit doctors to withdraw seed directly from the body via a needle.[184] Since such withdrawal of seed does not cause pleasure, it is permitted. We can similarly understand why Tosafos permit women to destroy seed, since women get no pleasure from such destruction. Moreover, we can understand the assertion of the *Chazon Ish*[185] that when one person causes a second person to willingly emit seed, only the second person, who experiences pleasure, transgresses the prohibition of *hotza'as zera le-vatalah*. The first person, who does not experience pleasure, does not transgress.

---

184. See *Otzar ha-Poskim*, ibid. p. 176.
185. Cited in *Otzar ha-Poskim*, ibid. p. 168.

Chapter 8

Man & Woman

The *Shulchan Aruch*[186] mentions two intentions one might have during intercourse: fulfilling Hashem's command of *peru u-revu* by procreating, and achieving immortality by procreating. The *Shulchan Aruch* endorses the former intention and cautions against the latter. Indeed, every husband has an inalienable right to pursue fulfillment of *peru u-revu*, and wives who interfere with this pursuit are deemed rebellious and penalized.[187] Yet while wives should concentrate during intercourse, like their husbands, on fulfilling Hashem's will,[188] the wife's right to children cannot stem, like the husband's, from Hashem's command of *peru u-revu*. After all, women are not subject to this commandment.[189] Rather, a wife's right to children stems from her desire for succor in old age, for dignity or immortality in death, or from her other emotional needs. This chapter will discuss various halakhic perspectives, some concrete and others abstract, on the source of a wife's right to children.

---

186. *Orach Chaim* 231.
187. *Shulchan Aruch, Even ha-Ezer* 154.
188. *Iggeres ha-Kodesh*, ch. 5.
189. *Yevamos* 65b.

Discussion of this topic begins with two talmudic passages that contradict or dispute one another regarding the scope of a woman's credibility to establish her husband's sterility. Do we believe a woman if she claims that her husband's seed "does not shoot like an arrow," i.e., lacks the motility necessary to impregnate her, or not? In *Yevamos*,[190] the Talmud assigns wives greater credibility, while in *Nedarim*,[191] the Talmud suspects them of falsely leveling this allegation in order to obtain a divorce and marry someone else. There are five resolutions to this contradiction, and each resolution yields a different perspective on why wives are entitled to children.

First, some Rishonim[192] suggest that we only believe the wife when divorce proceedings were already initiated by the husband or by the courts. Under these circumstances, when a divorce is already imminent, we are not concerned that she is leveling her allegation to obtain a divorce. According to this, the wife's unsubstantiated allegation can never result in a divorce.

Second, Tosafos[193] maintain that we believe the wife when the court knows by other means, such as medical records or the husband's admission, that the husband is sterile. According to this, too, the wife's unsubstantiated allegation can never win her freedom to pursue children with another man. However, this opinion does

---
190. Ibid.
191. 90b-91a.
192. See Meiri to *Yevamos* 65a.
193. *Yevamos* 65a, 65b.

emphasize the wife's right to children, since when the court knows that her husband cannot provide her with children, they compel him to divorce her.

Third, the Talmud[194] writes that we believe the wife when her request for children stems from a desire for "a cane for the hand and a shovel for burial." Tosafos[195] seem to interpret this as a desire for succor in old age and dignity in death. However, if she says her request stems from a desire for immortality, desire to avoid being "one who has no sons [and] is considered like dead," we deny her request, since she has no right to immortality. In contrast, the Netziv[196] writes that "a cane for the hand" refers to immortality, to "a cane for the hand *to memorialize my name.*" Hence, we believe her when she requests divorce for the sake of perpetuating her memory through offspring. However, we do not believe the wife when she requests divorce in order to fulfill *mitzvas peru u-revu*, since she is not subject to that mitzvah.

Fourth, R. Achai Gaon writes in his *She'iltos*[197] that we believe the wife when she requests only a divorce, but we do not believe her when she requests divorce and payment of her *kesubah*. The simple explanation of this is that the woman, by requesting *kesubah* payment and displaying an ulterior monetary motive, impugns her credibility. However, the Netziv[198] suggests that

---

194. Ibid. 65b.
195. Ibid. 65a.
196. *Ha'amek She'elah* to *She'ilta* 18, no. 11 (vol. 1, p. 116).
197. *She'ilta* 18.
198. *Ha'amek She'elah*, ibid. no. 7 (pp. 114-115).

women who focus solely on children, who ignore the *kesubah*, must be possessed by an all-consuming desire for children. Such women are entitled to the emotional comfort that they can only derive from hopeful pursuit of conception. In contrast, women who ask for *kesubah* money in the same breath as they request children possess a weaker desire for children. We can and do ensure such women emotional comfort by distracting them from their husbands' infertility, and thereby avoid the frightening necessity of compelling divorce.

Fifth, some Rishonim argue that we believe the wife if she requests divorce after ten years of marriage, but we do not believe her if she requests it sooner. What is the significance of this ten-year time span? The Talmud[199] writes that a couple must divorce if ten childless years have elapsed since that couple's marriage. The Vilna Gaon[200] adds that this obligation is still in force nowadays. However, they need not divorce immediately if either partner was ill or incarcerated at some time during the ten years. Rishonim[201] imply that the couple must divorce only if their infertility can be attributed to Hashem's inscrutable will, since such infertility, once it has lasted ten years, is likely to remain permanent. In contrast, the couple need not divorce if their infertility can be attributed to a confounding variable, such as illness, imprisonment, sin, or potentially curable physiological imbalances or imperfections.

---

199. *Yevamos* 64a.
200. *Even ha-Ezer* 1.
201. See Rosh, *Yevamos* 6:12.

For this reason, the Rashba[202] writes that if a couple relocated to Eretz Yisrael, they restart the ten-year count, since the merit of settling in Eretz Yisrael may help them have children. Similarly, if a couple starts a new course of treatment, they restart the ten-year count, since perhaps the new treatment will help them have children. Everyone agrees, however, that the couple must divorce if they sought no new merits or treatments during the ten years, even if such merits or treatments are available. As long as new hope awaits the couple over the horizon, as long as the couple believes in their own fertility, the ten-year count cannot begin; the countdown to divorce commences only when hope begins to be displaced by despair. Based on this, we can explain why the wife's allegation of her husband's infertility is only accepted after the ten years elapsed. The wife is entitled to hopeful pursuit of children, and during the ten years, *halakhah* indicates that she may, should, and must still hope. Only after ten years elapse does she lose the hope that is hers by right, and only then may she credibly sue for divorce.

To conclude, *halakhah* acknowledges and empathizes with couples experiencing the agony of infertility. It realizes that infertility can cause tension between spouses, either when one spouse is objectively known to be sterile, or, less legitimately, when one spouse simply supposes the other to be sterile. When legislating how to address such spousal conflict, *halakhah* emphasizes purity of intention:

---

202. *Yevamos* 64a.

we heed the wife's request when she is motivated by proper considerations, but not when she is motivated by improper considerations. Everyone agrees that a woman is not entitled to children for the purpose of fulfilling *peru u-revu*. Most opinions agree that she is entitled to children for succor in old age. Tosafos and the Netziv dispute whether or not she is entitled to children for perpetuating her memory. Yet other sources indicate that the wife is entitled to hope for children, to dream of children, and to look forward to children.

When infertility leads to tension, every possible course of action yields both tragedy and hope. Dissolution of a marriage is tragic, but it yields hope that each partner will succeed in procreating with a different spouse. Preservation of the marriage yields hope of peace and comfort, but leaves the couple vulnerable to the pain of constantly speculating, "will I have children?" The Mishnah,[203] sensitive to the tragic potential implicit in each course of action, advises the couple to "make a path of pleading." Tosafos[204] interpret: the couple should pray to Hashem for fertility, and have a romantic dinner to deepen their bonds of love. May Hashem grant all Jewish families love and fertility forever.

---

203. *Nedarim* 90b.
204. *Yevamos* 65a.

Chapter 9

Old & Young

Hashem commanded Adam, Noah, and Yaakov to "be fruitful and multiply" (*peru u-revu*).[205] Beis Hillel interpret that this command binds us, the descendants of its recipients, to exert ourselves to have children until we have one boy and one girl.[206] King Shlomo added: "in the morning sow your seeds and do not rest your hand in the evening (*la-erev al tanach yadecha*), for you do not know which will be suitable, this or that, or whether both will be equally good."[207] R. Yehoshua interprets that this verse binds us to exert ourselves to have children even after we have one boy and one girl.[208] To what extent do the parameters and themes of Hashem's command and King Shlomo's corollary dovetail, and to what extent do they diverge? There are four universally acknowledged distinctions between *peru u-revu* and *la-erev al tanach yadecha*, and five disputed distinctions. What are these distinctions, and what is their significance? This chapter, in the course of answering these questions, will

---

205. *Bereishis* 1:28, 9:1, 9:7, and 35:11.
206. *Yevamos* 61b.
207. *Koheles* 11:6.
208. *Yevamos* 62b.

analyze three teleological themes of *mitzvas peru u-revu* that emerge by way of contrast with "do not rest your hand in the evening."

Peru u-revu is a *mitzvah bein adam la-Makom* (between Hashem and man) or *bein adam le-chaveiro* (between one man and his fellow), an altruistic, other-directed mitzvah, an obligation of the individual towards his G-d and his nation. In contrast, *la-erev* is a *mitzvah bein adam le-atzmo* (between man and his inner self), a selfish obligation. We can reach this conclusion by means of the following analysis. R. Zerachyahu ha-Levi seems to maintain that the courts are authorized or obligated to compel a man to fulfill either of these *mitzvos*, using corporal force if necessary.[209] Ramban, however, argues that the courts may compel a person to fulfill *peru u-revu*, but once he has a boy and a girl, the courts may not compel him to father further children.[210] Ramban's position, which is endorsed by most Rishonim, indicates that *la-erev* is not mandatory, or at least not biblically mandatory. Had it been biblically mandatory, the courts would be obligated to compel its fulfillment, as they are obligated to compel fulfillment of other biblically mandatory *mitzvos*.[211]

Most Rishonim agree that *la-erev* is not mandatory, and they therefore rule that one who swears to violate *la-erev* must uphold his oath.[212] Similarly, since

---
209. *Ba'al ha-Ma'or* to Rif on *Yevamos* 19b-20a.
210. *Milchamos Hashem* to Rif, ibid..
211. See *Sedei Chemed*, vol. 3, pp. 110-117, 203-205.
212. See *Sedei Chemed*, vol. 2, pp. 286-288.

la-erev is voluntary, it is superseded by Rabbeinu Gershom's ban against polygamy.[213] Therefore, if a man already has a boy and a girl, and his wife becomes sterile, and it is halakhically difficult to divorce her, he may not marry a second wife in order to have further children. In contrast, the *Ohr Zarua* as interpreted by R. Yoel Sirkes[214] holds that *la-erev* is biblically mandatory, and therefore the oath of one who swears to violate *la-erev* is null and void, just like the oath of one who swears to violate any biblical mitzvah. Similarly, some Poskim maintain that one may marry a second wife to have further children if one's first wife became sterile while he was unable to divorce her.[215] R. Sirkes' opinion leads to the following problem: if *la-erev* is biblically mandatory, and the courts are obligated to compel fulfillment of biblically mandatory obligations, why are the courts not obligated to compel fulfillment of *la-erev*?

To resolve this difficulty, we must reanalyze the significance of Ramban's ruling that courts cannot compel fulfillment of *la-erev*. Perhaps Ramban's position indicates that the recalcitrant man's refusal to fulfill the biblical mitzvah of *la-erev* does not hurt Hashem and the Jewish nation to the same extent as refusal to fulfill other biblical *mitzvos*. Therefore, the court, as an agent of Hashem and of the Jewish collective, has less authority to compel its fulfillment.

---

213. See *Otzar ha-Poskim* vol. 1, p. 31.
214. *Bayis Chadash, Yoreh Deah* 228.
215. See *Otzar ha-Poskim*, ibid.

In contrast, one who neglects *peru u-revu* is derelict in his biblically mandatory obligation towards Hashem and towards the Jews; therefore, the courts can compel him to perform *mitzvas peru u-revu*.

The idea that *peru u-revu* is an altruistic, outward-directed mitzvah while *la-erev al tanach yadecha* is a selfish, inward-directed mitzvah finds expression in other sources. For instance, the Raavad[216] writes that *la-erev* is only "good advice," but is not a bona fide Torah value. For this reason, Raavad maintains that one who already fathered a boy and a girl may marry a sterile woman. Similarly, even the Ramban, who forbids a father of children from marrying a sterile woman, believes that *la-erev* alone does not imbue the pursuit of further children with axiological valence; only coupled with the divine desire for the world to be well-populated does *la-erev* render pursuit of further children valuable. Moreover, King Shlomo's language indicates that *la-erev's* focus is inwards. "You do not know which will be suitable, this or that," which set of children will survive, which will make you most proud, which will live close to your home and succor you in old age, and which will bring you more merits in heaven through their performance of righteous deeds. This is King Shlomo's message: have children *for your own sake*, for your own immortality, your own comfort, and your own merit.

A second set of distinctions indicates that prior to fulfilling *peru u-revu*, marriage is primarily about

---

216. *Hasagos* to *Ba'al ha-Ma'or*, ibid.

producing children, while once a man has fulfilled *peru u-revu*, even though he must still fulfill *la-erev*, his marriage is primarily about love, respect, dignity, and decency. To clarify, this does not mean that a person may ever fight with his or her spouse about having children. Fighting with one's spouse is biblically forbidden. Moreover, such fights are counterproductive, and hardly ever contribute to fulfilling *peru u-revu*. Love, respect, dignity, and decency must form the bedrock of marriage even before *peru u-revu* is fulfilled. The consensus of opinions is that the sources cited in the following paragraphs apply in a limited range of circumstances, and the reader is advised not to generalize and assume that they have any practical relevance to his or her circumstances.

The Mishnah[217] writes that a sterile woman married to a childless man may not drink the *sotah* waters, which restore harmony and completion to a marriage by clarifying whether or not the wife was faithful to her husband, while a sterile woman married to a father of children must drink those waters. The *Mishneh le-Melech*[218] rejects the possibility that this law is a rabbinic decree to encourage procreation, or that it is a result of the husband's sin of cohabiting with a sterile woman. Rather, he favors Rashi's interpretation that the sterile woman may not drink *sotah* waters because her marriage is on a trajectory towards dissolution, as the courts will compel her husband to divorce her

---
217. *Sotah* 26a.
218. *Hilchos Sotah* 2:10.

so that he can fulfill *peru u-revu*. Similarly, Rambam[219] writes that the Torah explicitly excludes sterile women from drinking *sotah* waters, presumably because their marriages cannot fulfill their husbands' halakhically mandated reproductive drive. The *sotah* waters are not meant to restore a marriage that was flawed from its outset. Only when the husbands' reproductive drive is satisfied, when *peru u-revu* is already fulfilled, or is able to be fulfilled, when the emphasis of marriage shifts away from children and towards promoting love and harmony, can we deem the sterile woman's marriage complete. Only such a marriage can be restored to completion by the *sotah* waters.

Along similar lines, ten years after a childless couple ceases to seek new methods to conceive, the courts must compel them to divorce. In contrast, once the husband has children, even if he and his wife remain childless for ten years, the courts do not compel them to divorce.[220] R. Zerachyahu ha-Levi explains that *peru u-revu* is a bona fide obligation, and hence overrides our reluctance to compel a divorce. *Peru u-revu* is more important than nurturing love between spouses. In contrast, *la-erev* belongs to the realm of *derekh eretz*, of civility and dignity, of love and harmony. Therefore, the spouses' love for each other and desire to stay together overrides the obligation of *la-erev al tanach yadecha*. For this reason, the *Terumas ha-Deshen*[221] rules

---
219. Commentary on Mishnayos to *Sotah* 4:3.
220. *Yevamos* 64a.
221. 1:264.

that a father of children may forego marrying a fertile but quarrelsome woman, and instead marry a sterile but peaceful woman. Once he has children, the objective of marriage is peace and harmony. Yet a childless man must marry a fertile woman, even if she is quarrelsome, and may not marry a peaceful sterile woman. As long as the reproductive drive is unfulfilled, peace is only a secondary telos in marriage.

Another proof for this thesis may be adduced from the laws of mourning. A father of children whose wife passed away may not marry until three holidays have passed. Within the three-holiday period, we are concerned that the widower's memories of his deceased wife will detrimentally impact on his ability to succor and to harmoniously interact with his new wife. Since he already has children, harmonious interaction is his primary goal in marriage. In contrast, a childless man may marry almost immediately after his wife's passing, even though it will be hard from him to harmoniously interact with his second wife. Since he has not yet fulfilled *peru u-revu*, satisfying the halakhic procreative drive takes priority, and ensuring maximum harmony may be somewhat compromised.

The final and most controversial distinction between *peru u-revu* and *la-erev* concerns the permissibility of selling a Torah scroll to finance marriage. All authorities agree that one may sell a scroll to finance the marriage of a childless man to a fertile woman, since such marriage is a precursor to *peru u-revu*. Yet the Raavad maintains that one may not sell a scroll to allow a father of children to marry a fertile woman; better leave the scroll unsold and have him marry a sterile woman. In contrast, Ramban maintains that one must sell a scroll to facilitate even a father of children's marriage to a fertile woman, since he has yet to fulfill the mitzvah of *la-erev*.

Some opinions suggest that for Ramban, both *peru u-revu* and *la-erev* facilitate the transmission of Torah more than possession of a Torah scroll. These *mitzvos* mandate not only perpetuation of the father's DNA, but perpetuation of his spiritual legacy. To quote R. Hershel Schachter:[222]

> ... the whole mitzva of *piryah v'rivya* is for the purpose of perpetuating klal yisroel, the ultimate purpose of which is *masores ha-Torah*, passing Torah from one generation to the next....

For this reason, one may delay *peru u-revu* in order to acquire greater familiarity with Torah concepts and greater ability to pass them on. Such a delay does not constitute neglect of *peru u-revu;* rather, it constitutes a critical prerequisite for the proper fulfillment of *peru u-revu*. Similarly, one who imbues adopted children with Torah values,[223] and one who supports *yeshivos* that

---

222. "Halakhic Aspects of Family Planning," *Journal of Halakhah and Contemporary Society* IV (1985), p. 15, fn. 36
223. *Chochmas Shlomo, Even ha-Ezer* 1:1.

impart Torah values to their students[224] has partially fulfilled the mitzvah of *peru u-revu*. In contrast, the Raavad may believe that *peru u-revu* alone is thematically bound to transmission of Torah values, while *la-erev* is primarily a piece of good advice, a voluntary mitzvah, or a *mitzvah bein adam le-atzmo*. Hence, retaining possession of the Torah scroll, an act that lends dignity to Torah and facilitates the owner's study and fulfillment of Torah, should not be displaced by *la-erev*, which is unrelated thematically to perpetuation of Torah. One must teach Torah values to all his children, but this obligation is distinct from the mitzvah of *la-erev*.

In conclusion, we return to our original question: to what extent do the parameters and themes of *peru u-revu* dovetail with those of *la-erev*, and to what extent do they diverge? In other words, to what extent are *peru u-revu* and *la-erev* a single, integrated mitzvah, and to what extent are they distinct *mitzvos*? We have seen that *peru u-revu* is certainly a biblical *mitzvah*, while *la-erev* may be only rabbinic or only "good advice." Moreover, *peru u-revu* justifies a greater degree of judicial compulsion, both for bachelors and for couples who have given up on having children, while *la-erev* does not justify such compulsion. In addition, the importance of *peru u-revu* overrides halakhic concerns about guarding harmony and retaining ownership of Torah scrolls, while *la-erev* does not necessarily override such concerns. Hence, despite the fact that many of these

---

224. *Kisvei Chofetz Chaim*, cited by R. Schachter, ibid.

laws where *la-erev* differs from *peru u-revu* are disputed, it appears that the parameters and themes of these *mitzvos* diverge, and that they are independent and distinct from one another.

Chapter 10

Jew & Gentile

Ritual law is a distinct entity from civil law. R. Nissim[225] writes that the purpose of ritual laws, such as the laws governing sacrificial service, is to unfold Hashem's influence in our midst. Enforcement of these laws is the exclusive domain of Jewish courts. In contrast, the purpose of civil laws, such as those governing the prohibition against murder, is to maintain a just society. Enforcement of these laws is the domain of the king, or, among gentiles, the government. R. Nissim's analysis yields the conclusion that laws pertaining to gentiles necessarily belong to the civil domain, while laws pertaining exclusively to Jews may belong to the ritual domain. Although R. Yisroel Gustman[226] has convincingly demonstrated that a single mitzvah may have different parameters with regard to Jews and gentiles, we will assume that, nevertheless, any mitzvah classified as civil with regard to gentiles can be classified as civil with regard to Jews as well. This chapter will discuss whether the verses "be fruitful and

---
225. *Derashos ha-Ran* 11.
226. *Kuntresei Shiurim* to *Bava Metzia* pp. 85-96.

multiply"[227] (*peru u-revu*) and "Hashem did not create the world for emptiness; He created it to be settled"[228] (*lo tohu bera'ah, le-sheves yetzarah*), and the obligations deriving therefrom, are primarily designed to maintain society and perpetuate the nation or species, or primarily designed to help Hashem's presence unfold in our midst.

The Rambam issued a number of anomalous rulings that blur the line between *peru u-revu* and *sheves*, and indicate that both are civil rather than ritual laws. First, the Rambam[229] implies that women are exempt from *sheves* just as they are exempt from *peru u-revu*. Second, where a Mishnah[230] states that servants are bound to fulfill *sheves*, the Rambam[231] paraphrases that servants are bound to fulfill *peru u-revu*. Third, the *Mabit*[232] writes that gentiles are obligated in *peru u-revu*. The Rambam[233] may agree with the *Mabit*, as he rules that a convert whose children also converted has fulfilled *peru u-revu*, while a convert whose children remain gentiles has not fulfilled *peru u-revu*. Somehow, having children *as a gentile*, if subsequent events unfold in a particular fashion, is sufficient to fulfill *peru u-revu*.

---

227. *Bereishis* 1:28, 9:1, 9:7, and 35:11.
228. *Yeshaya* 45:18.
229. *Hilchos Ishus* 15:16, and *Hilchos Issurei Bi'ah* 21:26, as interpreted by R. Moshe Trachtman, *Ma'aseh Choshev*, mitzvah 1, p. 80.
230. *Gittin* 41b.
231. *Hilchos Avadim* 7:7.
232. See *Encyclopedia Talmudit*, vol. 3, p. 395.
233. *Hilchos Ishus* 15:6.

Acharonim question both the logic and the source of this ruling. In defense of the Rambam's logic, R. Eliakim Koenigsberg[234] writes that *mitzvas peru u-revu* obligates us to perpetuate the Jewish nation. It follows from R. Koenigsberg's reasoning that *mitzvas peru u-revu* obligates each gentile to perpetuate the nation to which he or she belongs. Hence, when the convert and his children were gentiles, he was in fulfillment of his mitzvah, and when he and his children converted, he remained in fulfillment of his mitzvah. Based on this, we can also adduce a source for the Rambam. The Talmud Yerushalmi[235] writes that a Jewish man who has a child with a gentile woman has not fulfilled *peru u-revu*, since the child is not Jewish, but rather belongs to its mother's nation. This indicates that one only fulfills *peru u-revu* through a child who belongs to his nation, perhaps because the mitzvah obligates each man to perpetuate specifically his nation.

Like the Rambam, Tosafos[236] link *peru u-revu* and *sheves*. Unlike the Rambam, however, Tosafos[237] classify these *mitzvos* as ritual laws rather than civil laws. Hence, Tosafos write that gentiles are neither obligated in *peru u-revu* nor in *sheves*. However, most Rishonim reject this opinion of Tosafos, and Tosafos themselves proffer alternate opinions.

---

234. *Kuntres He'aros* to *Yevamos*, p. 139.
235. *Yevamos* 2:6.
236. *Yevamos* 62a.
237. Ibid.

Tosafos[238] alternatively suggest that gentiles and servants are exempt from *peru u-revu*, but still obligated in *sheves*. Tosafos understand that *sheves* obligates man to perpetuate his species. Hence, a convert whose children are gentiles has fulfilled the mitzvah of *sheves*, since he helped perpetuate the human species. However, gentiles and servants are not obligated in *peru u-revu*. Hence, the Talmud Yerushalmi[239] rules that servants may postpone their weddings until the holidays and then get married on a holiday, since servants are only obligated in *sheves*, and fulfillment of *sheves* is not urgent and therefore may be delayed. In contrast, since Jews are obligated in *peru u-revu*, they may not marry on holidays, lest they delay fulfillment of *peru u-revu* in order to have their weddings coincide with the holiday.

R. Daniel Wolff[240] finds echoes of this distinction between *peru u-revu* and *sheves* in other rulings of the Tosafos. For instance, Tosafos[241] seem to rule that one may not free his half-servant, half-freedman—who cannot marry on account of his split status—for the sake of *peru u-revu*, but one may not free that servant in order for the servant to fulfill *sheves*. This is because keeping a servant properly is a ritual mitzvah, and will cause the divine presence to unfold with equal efficacy to *mitzvas peru u-revu*. However, only by freeing the servant will the master help the human species perpetuate; therefore, the master must free his servant.

---

238. *Chagigah* 2b.
239. *Mo'ed Katan* 1:7.
240. *Minchah le-Aharon*, pp. 50-52.
241. *Bava Basra* 13a.

Based on this, R. Wolff explains why the master may violate his mitzvah to keep the servant for the sake of the servant's fulfillment of *peru u-revu*. Ordinarily, we do not allow one person to sin for the purpose of providing a different person with merit. Here, however, the master's actions too contribute to the perpetuation of humanity, since without his participation the servant would be unable to help perpetuate humanity. Hence he is not sinning for his servant's merit, but for his own merit, and such sins are sometimes permitted.

Conclusion

Peru u-revu is neither an isolated mitzvah nor a simple one. On the one hand, *peru u-revu* plays a central role in the mitzvah of marriage, as well as in the prohibitions against *sirus*, *hotza'as zera le-vatalah*, and intermarriage between ancestral Jews and *mamzerim*. Indeed, its impact may spread well beyond the limited *mitzvos* and prohibitions discussed in this book, touching, among others, the mitzvah to marry third-generation Egyptian and Edomite converts and the prohibition for eunuchs (*petzuah daka* and *kerus shafcha*) to marry.

Yet on the other hand, *peru u-revu* is hardly monochromatic. Rather, it comes in many hues, from *sheves*, to *la-erev al tanach yadecha*, to ordinary *peru u-revu*. *Peru u-revu* is the antidote to the most primal fear of the human racce, the fear of eternal oblivion; it is the "cane for the hand" and the "shovel for burial." In its fulfillment, people may partake of one of the greatest physical pleasures. The constellation of *mitzvos* of which *peru u-revu* is a part acknowledges our fear and our desire. It acknowledges that our fear is Hashem's fear, for "He did not create it for oblivion," and our desire is Hashem's desire, for "He created the world to be settled." Yet precisely because Hashem created us to share His will, He can and does call upon us to subsume our will to His will. He calls upon us to act with discipline and with noble intentions. And in this, His *halakhah* faithfully reflects the challenges of the human experience, portrays for us the heights that life can reach, and guides us ever upwards from exalted peak to exalted peak.

Index

Talmud

Berachos 10a, 20, 41

Shabbos 54a, 64
Shabbos 110b, 64
Shabbos 111a, 64-66

Chagigah 2b, 93

Yevamos 12b, 36, 69
Yevamos 16b, 33
Yevamos 34a, 42
Yevamos 34b, 56, 68, 70, 72
Yevamos 53b, 54
Yevamos 55a, 56
Yevamos 55b, 53, 59
Yevamos 56a, 54
Yevamos 57b, 41
Yevamos 59b, 61
Yevamos 60b, 42
Yevamos 61b, 20, 57, 80
Yevamos 62a, 21, 50, 52, 92
Yevamos 62b, 29, 80
Yevamos 63a, 44
Yevamos 63b, 21-22, 44, 50
Yevamos 64a, 22, 77, 85
Yevamos 65a, 75-76, 79

Yevamos 65b, 45, 74, 75-76
Yevamos 90b-91a, 75

Nedarim 20b, 70
Nedarim 90b, 79

Sotah 2a, 39
Sotah 26a, 84

Gittin 41b, 911

Kiddushin 7a, 47
Kiddushin 42a, 45, 49
Kiddushin 78a, 56

Bava Basra 13a, 93
Bava Basra 56b, 39

Sanhedrin 55b, 42
Sanhedrin 68b-69a, 36
Sanhedrin 69b, 37
Sanhedrin 68b, 37
Sanhedrin 69a, 37, 43
Sanhedrin 69b, 42
Sanhedrin 70b, 57

Bechoros 45b, 29

Kerisos 19b, 57

Rambam

Ishus 3:21-22, 48
Ishus 10:7, 48
Ishus 10:9, 48
Ishus 12:6-8, 48
Ishus 15:1, 47
Ishus 15:2, 22-23
Ishus 15:3, 23
Ishus 15:16, 91

Issurei Bi'ah 12:1, 13
Issurei Bi'ah 15:2, 33
Issurei Bi'ah 21:1, 60
Issurei Bi'ah 21:18, 69
Issurei Bi'ah 21:26, 91

Avadim 7:7, 91

Shulchan Aruch

Orach Chaim 307:16, 71

Even ha-Ezer 1:3, 20
Even ha-Ezer 1:4, 23
Even ha-Ezer 2:7, 29
Even ha-Ezer 5:11, 64
Even ha-Ezer 5:12-13, 66
Even ha-Ezer 5:13, 65

www.ingramcontent.com/pod-product-compliance
Lightning Source LLC
Chambersburg PA
CBHW051707040426
42446CB00008B/767